MW00977140

Beyond Money

Timeless Wisdom for Financial Wellness

Brad Rosley, CFP®

Free Bonus

This book includes a FREE blueprint

"Financial Wellness: Everyone Deserves a Financial Plan"
Click Here to Download or go to
www.RKFinancialWellness.com/free

Beyond Money
All rights reserved © 2018

Although the author and publisher have made every effort to ensure that the information in this book was correct at press time, the author and publisher do not assume and hereby disclaim any liability to any party for any loss, damage, or disruption caused by errors or omissions, whether such errors or omissions result from negligence, accident, or any other cause.

ISBN-13: 978-1720678663
ISBN-10: 1720678669

Dedication

———— ∽ ————

My parents absolute love and their examples, are my inspirations for this book.

I thank my mother, Joyce, for setting an amazing example of how to live life generously and selflessly. Her unconditional love and support have always been my rock. Her frugal ways taught me well and sent me in the right direction both personally and professionally.

My father, Howard, also set a great example for me by living a balanced lifestyle, not waiting until retirement to do the things he wanted to do like golf all the time and fish. Although I was devastated when he passed away at the young age of 58, his dying so young greatly influenced my "balanced living" approach to financial planning. I am blessed to have learned so much from my father, whose teachings are the foundations of my business and how I raise my own family. Some of my closest friends nicknamed me "Howard" and still call me that today. I'm grateful for that. I miss him every day, but I know he watches my family from Heaven with pride and unending love.

My wife, Soni, doesn't have a formal financial background, but the way she was raised and the thrifty qualities she brought to our marriage have served our family well. I love her for the support she has always given my career and am thankful to have married such a terrific woman.

Lastly, I was inspired to write this book in large part for my three amazing children, Jake, Olivia, and Isabella. Though they are teenagers and are at an age where they don't readily accept my words of wisdom, I am hopeful that one day they will. This book was written as a financial wellness guide for their benefit. If they don't—or can't—ever ask me directly about their financial issues, I hope they will refer to this book to guide them as it is all about what I did with my finances for the betterment of our family's financial wellbeing.

Table of contents

My Mission

———— ⌘ ————

I had known for a long time that working in the financial industry was my calling, and I began my careful studies during college majoring in finance. In 1996, I started my financial advisory practice, Fortune Financial Group, Inc.

I have been blessed with success—in both my career and, even more importantly, in my personal life. It is because of my wife and children that I have learned that the goal of my personal work is overall financial wellness. I believe the term, wellness, incorporates a stronger, more holistic goal. Financial wellness is not simplistic; it cannot be quantified, because it's beyond just the numbers in your bank accounts. It is beyond just the market value of your home.

It is *Beyond Money*.

In my experience, both in my personal life and as an advisor to many clients over more than two decades, money is nothing more than a tool. It is a tool to carve out a path towards your life's priorities. My own priorities surround my

Family, my Faith, and my Friends. These Capital Fs are the goal, and to meet these I use my lower-case-f tool: finances.

Your life's priorities are unique, and I have helped many people and families meet their priorities with my financial guidance. It is my firm belief that when you take action by prioritizing your goals and using appropriate strategies, tailored to your situation, your life will truly be better for it.

Financial wellness is having full confidence in your situation so it's not a source of stress. Financial wellness means you can focus your energy on achieving your goals.

Financial wellness begins with having a financial plan and it must be a personalized financial plan. I have done this for myself and for my clients, and I have done so successfully.

February 2018 was a frightening month for many people who are invested in the stock market, the Dow Jones in particular. In the first two weeks of the month. the Dow plummeted 3,200 points, a 12 percent dip. Although it rallied, it crashed 680 points in the last two days of the month. Financial news of all varieties was clouded in fear, with scores of people wondering whether there was a risk of a major crisis.

None of my clients had this fear.

My phone did not ring one time with someone on the other end frightened about the state of their stock portfolio. Each client and I had developed a clear, personalized financial plan that gave them confidence that their financial wellness, their life beyond money, was not in jeopardy due to the market drop.

I wrote this book because I want to positively affect the lives of people beyond those clients I am lucky to meet with one-on-one. I want *everyone to have a financial plan* and the peace of mind that comes with it. There are many Americans who are living paycheck to paycheck, and just because someone is not does not mean that he or she is making wise financial decisions. There are problems that cross all income levels: from not enough money, health care, retirement, children's college funds, home-ownership, or simply the stress of the unknown.

Financial planning and creating the individual financial wellness I advocate in this book, addresses these problems clearly. Everyone—regardless of age, of income, of net worth—can learn to use the guidance in this book in one or more area of life to make it significantly better.

My colleagues and I have created a new company, RKFinancial Wellness (RK) with a broad mission:

Everyone Deserves a Financial Plan

We know the financial woes that many people face: not enough money to pay this month's bills; weighty credit card or student loan debt (sometimes both); and the anxiety of living paycheck to paycheck. Because of the vast number of people whose lives beyond money are dampened by these problems, RK wants to touch the lives of as many people as possible and bring financial health to readers beyond those people with whom we meet in-person. We hope the tools and strategies found inside these pages will unlock a path to financial wellness and will help you tackle any financial burden life throws your way.

RK's work goes beyond in-person meetings and this book. We know that engaging with a Certified Financial Planner can be intimidating and expensive for many people. Therefore, we are offering a tool that is confidential, customized, and inexpensive. This tool is to engage with employers to have them offer financial wellness as an employee benefit, either paid for by the employer or as a voluntary payroll deduction. RK Financial Wellness provides tools and strategies to help employees' lives Beyond Money, and we hope your employer will consider adding financial wellness as an employee benefit.

Prologue

———— ✌ ————

Steve Taylor had less than a month to live.

At 48, this was not when he had "planned" to go. But the cancer that had invaded his liver had other plans.

After Steve's diagnosis was delivered to him and his wife, Nancy, the typical feelings of shock and denial were the first emotions to well up inside his gut. He moved beyond that first stage, and shock gave way to pure anger. He knew that he would soon be released from the hospital and into hospice. During those last few days at the hospital, his anger waned. He was left with a new and very dark feeling.

Regret.

For all his life, Steve had been the man to whom people would go for getting things done. With over 27 years as an employee of RT Industries, he had taken the typical corporate ride from a junior sales representative to manager of the entire sales force of 106 representatives in fewer than six years. At 42, he had been promoted to Senior VP of the entire division.

The past six years had been full of challenges: company growth and late nights at the office—maybe too many.

He had purchased life insurance, was fully funded in his company's 401k, and was able to set aside a meager amount of money for college for his three children. The taxman had taken his share, and his wife had to work part-time. But the family was ok financially—or so he thought.

Now, as he was dying, an excruciating emotional pain was taking over.

The current regret—the one that ate at his gut worse than the cancer— was one people often don't take action on to prevent. The regret is one we all know about, talk about, but rarely do anything about because we think we can fix the problem later.

Ask any wise old person what matters most, and they rarely speak about their home, their material possessions, or their career. When you ask seasoned senior citizens, what's the most valuable thing in life, most people say the same thing:

"What matters most is spending time with those we love."

Period.

As Steve was dying, he worried that he hadn't focused on spending time with those whom he loved most.

Steve was a good provider and, by his estimation, a good father to his three children. Katie, his eldest, was only in the 9th grade and already looking at the University of Illinois. His son, Jack, was about to enter junior high school. His youngest, Sara, was a precocious nine-year-old who loved to catch bugs; she just wasn't that into school.

He knew that his premature death would be tough on all of them.

His kids loved him, and the regret that tore at his soul was lacking the only thing that truly mattered: Time with his wife and kids.

Facing such a quick death created a flash of images of things he would never experience.

No walking Katie down the aisle for her wedding. No bouncing a grandchild in his lap, listening to the hypnotic laughter of an infant. No vacation to Greece when he became an empty-nester like he and his wife had dreamed and talked about.

"Damn it!" He shouted a bit too loudly.

It was 2 a.m., and he couldn't sleep. He buzzed the nurse for a cup of tea. As he patiently waited, his mind drifted to his home. In his mind's eye, he passed through the hallway into the kitchen; family photos on the credenza loomed up at him in the dim light of the nightlight taunting him like demons—like the demon he now feared he had become.

The phrase "If only" was consistently spinning around his head, even when he tried to think of other things.

"If only I had taken the family on that road trip we spoke about."

"If only I could live long enough to chaperone Katie's dance her senior year of high school."

"If only I had decided to coach Jack's softball team."

"If only..."

Introduction

Steve Taylor may be a fictional character in this book, but his story is, sadly, all too common. Most of us believe it will never happen to us, dying at a young age and with a young family. We purchase insurance and save a little bit "just in case," because, even though we don't believe it will happen to us, we have a bit of fear that the unexpected might happen.

That's a fear that comes up in the back of our minds every day.

As a Certified Financial Planner, I am one of the few financial specialists who focuses on more than just finances.

"Say what?"

You see, I think of money as just paper; money does not give us peace of mind, security, or the deep-seated things we crave. Account balances on a statement don't buy happiness. If money were indeed the key to happiness, would so many wealthy couples divorce or have dysfunctional families?

It may be different for you. But, no matter what drives you or gives you purpose, I guarantee it is not money. You may think it is money, though.

So, what does drive you? What is "it?"

Your true motivation, your purpose as a person, is very personal and unique. Few people know what it is early in life. Some realize it after a near-death experience. For those fortunate enough to "have" a death bed, their purpose is crystal clear.

Money is not it. What money can sometimes do, however, is create opportunities for your true motivation. But not all the time.

Recently, I was on a mission trip to Mexico and was having dinner with the family who hosted the trip. These people were poor, but only financially.

Their home had a dirt floor. Their kids each had one pair of shoes, and there was no flat screen TV, savings account, or air conditioning.

They had nothing materially.

But they had something I did not have.

After spending four hours with them one night, a realization hit me like a ton of bricks. I was envious. I was intoxicated by a new wealth I had not seen so clearly in my entire life. The wealth this family had was priceless and, in fact, not able to be purchased for any sum of money.

They had joy.

Pure, authentic, and ear-to-ear grinning joy.

We ate at their table, chatting for hours, and I laughed with them the entire time. The joy they shared and the happiness they exuded amongst the dirt and lack of modern amenities were invigorating.

When was the last time you laughed for four hours straight?

I guarantee you this family did this nearly every day, which begs the question: Who is richer: the man who is stressed out, anxious, and even slightly miserable but who has a lot of money, or this family I met in Mexico?

If you had to choose between a poor existence filled with daily joy or having all the money you need to live extravagantly but being miserable, which would you choose?

"I'd find a way to be happy with the money!" I hear you say.

That's great. But you may have missed the point.

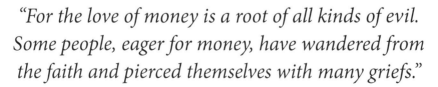

"For the love of money is a root of all kinds of evil. Some people, eager for money, have wandered from the faith and pierced themselves with many griefs."

Timothy 6:10

By now, you may have guessed: I'm not just about money. Money is only a tool. But there are dozens of tools that you must wield and become proficient in in order to create a life you truly desire.

Inside these pages, I will reference things, instruments if you will, like lifestyle, mortgages, insurance, and even spending habits. Like an orchestra, each of these instruments has a single, pure sound in the music it makes. Most financial professionals are proficient with one or more of these instruments. My training and worldview, however, mean I have a unique proficiency across the entire orchestra.

Like any professional musician, focusing on your core skills is certainly a good idea. Proficiency creates expertise. In your case, however, I'm suggesting you not attempt to become an expert in investing, mutual funds, insurance, or taxes. You could spend a lifetime in any of these areas and still be on a continuous learning curve.

Instead, I'd like to make you the conductor.

The conductor of an orchestra does not need to be proficient in every single instrument; he often does not want to be, either. He understands each instrument. He can detect the sound of a missed clarinet note amid the resounding volume of the entire symphony. He can hear if any of the instruments are out of tune. His real expertise, therefore, is in the blending of all the instruments.

Inside these pages, you'll begin to understand the way certain financial tools—beautiful musical instruments—interact. You will begin to understand the music of the orchestra.

I will give you strategies and tips on many of the individual instruments, but the focus and underlying theme of your financial intelligence will be built upon something other than finances. Your foundation of success is to be built with an important aspiration—an overall lifestyle that will present opportunities for joy and happiness in quality time with your loved ones, not expensive purchases.

The best things in life cannot be purchased.

This book is about more than just financial planning; it's about financial wellness. It's about creating and focusing on your life goals and then aligning your fiscal habits to reach for those goals. It's about financial strategies—some simple, others more complicated—that will help you gain financial control over your life.

I've been a Certified Financial Planner since 1990, and I've become rather proficient in my work. You will read about what I've learned throughout my career and believe to be the best strategies to succeed both financially and in life. I know a lot about making money, keeping money, and planning for a successful financial future, so I can tell you with all confidence: Life is not about money.

Money is a tool—a medium of exchange—not a purpose.

All too often we spend far too much time acquiring this tool, but then we forget what its purpose should actually be. I will teach you and remind you: Money's purpose is to help us act upon the truth that life is about living to the fullest and obtaining your dreams. To live life to the fullest and obtain your dreams, you *do* need financial planning to sharpen and use this tool, money. But the tool is not the end goal; the type of financial planning I confidently teach you will help you balance your life in the now with what you need to save for later. You shouldn't have to spend your time worrying about how you're going to get to your dreams. Time is better spent actually *being* there.

Money is a precious commodity, but time is irreplaceable. Once it's been used, it's not coming back. Our time in this life is short enough as it is; we don't need to waste it by spending most of it worrying about money.

As I've explained, the story of Steve Taylor is fictional. But don't be misled. Steve Taylor's thoughts, experiences, and circumstances are happening right now and to hundreds of thousands of people. I will use his story in this book to give you context and meaning to an otherwise dry topic about money; I can teach through Steve Taylor's story because this tool for teaching reflects *my* story.

My father left this world when he was only 58-years-old.

My father, like Steve, spent his life working to give us a better life. Sadly, he was diagnosed with cancer shortly before his retirement. His death was arguably the single most significant—and tragic—event in my life. It made me realize I needed to focus on what truly matters.

Premature death is not an uncommon story. We may plan for it in the form of insurance, but we rarely plan for it when investing our time. Many people work like a dog up until their retirement and then attempt to begin enjoying their life. That's when they realize there's not too much of life left at that point.

There has to be a better way.

My father's death made me realize that we have to focus far less on irrelevant financial points. What is "irrelevant?" The answer is relative to your situation. It took a major-medical issue in my family to drive home the fact of what was really important in *my* life. It wasn't watching sports, or losing a golf game, the weather, or even what's happening on the news in some far away part of the world. All that is designed to distract me. What is important to me is my family, those friends and neighbors who help me out, the ambitions my kids have, my Faith, and following through on the ambitions that I had as a kid. Nothing else truly matters. All the little extras I once spent my hard-earned money on were only holding me back, keeping me from helping my family and friends. Keeping me from achieving my goals.

It shouldn't take a major personal issue to set you on the right path. It shouldn't take impending death—especially your own—for you to realize how much time you've wasted by not really living. Stop living like you're merely filling time, but rather—as the Tim McGraw song says— "live like you were dying". This singular thought will help put you on the road to success and happiness.

The road to personal improvement and success is a never-ending journey. People tend to think in terms of beginnings and endings. The reality is that achieving our goals is merely the first step. The next step is to set a new goal and continue on with getting more out of ourselves and our lives. Once you realize this, then the whole "work for 30 years from 9 to 5 every day then retire for maybe five years of enjoyment" seems pointless. You've just spent 30 years working at something that is not actually your goal and that may well be completely irrelevant to that goal.

How would you plan your day if you thought you only had one year of good health left? What time and money wasters would you eliminate? Who would you be with? How much of your time and money would be spent working towards meaningful goals instead of using this tool to pay off that new big screen television you didn't really need? I've no doubt you would very quickly pare it all down to what really matters most.

This is the point from which I begin as a financial planner.

What matters most to you?

Money can get us a lot of things, but the accumulation of bigger numbers on an account statement is not true wealth. In most cases, relationships are our primary goals. Once that is clearly established we can design a financial plan that allows money to do what it does best: Provide peace of mind.

Once our true goals are aligned (and, yes, monetized), we can orchestrate a symphony of true prosperity. Your income, stocks, savings, lifestyle, habits, and goals will each become instruments being played in this symphony, and with my help, you will be its conductor.

A conductor of the music of life, meaning, and purpose.

The people who invest the time and deep thought into figuring out their true priorities and align their finances get the most out of life.

Highlights

- Money needs a purpose, a blueprint to help ensure it gets used to fulfill your unique life priorities.

- Most people don't take the time to examine their priorities, so they don't have a plan to use as a compass to help guide their decisions, financial and otherwise. Without a plan, they blow in the wind, subjecting themselves to impulse spending on very low priority items.

- Spending quality time with the people you love should rank at the top of your priorities. Arrange your finances so you can figure out a way to maximize that time.

Chapter One

Lifestyle

"There is very little correlation between income and happiness."

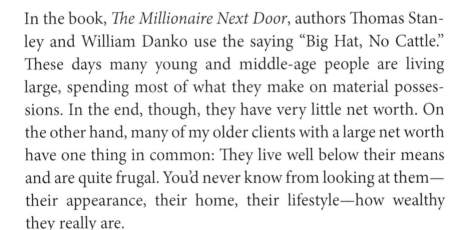

In the book, *The Millionaire Next Door*, authors Thomas Stanley and William Danko use the saying "Big Hat, No Cattle." These days many young and middle-age people are living large, spending most of what they make on material possessions. In the end, though, they have very little net worth. On the other hand, many of my older clients with a large net worth have one thing in common: They live well below their means and are quite frugal. You'd never know from looking at them—their appearance, their home, their lifestyle—how wealthy they really are.

The one great measure of true wealth is this: How long could you go without a paycheck? With roughly 75 percent of Americans living paycheck to paycheck, the answer for most is about one month.

You are where you are today in large part because of the decisions you have made throughout your life. Yes, many of us had setbacks that we had no control over. However, you *can* make changes going forward. Being aware of this fact is an integral part of the process.

The first step to creating a tuneful symphony out of the disharmony of your finances is to take a good, hard look at your lifestyle. Remember: You're supposed to be chasing goals, not possessions. A higher standard of living does not always equate to a higher *quality* of living. Compare what you want versus what you really *need*. In short, does what you pay out to maintain your current lifestyle match up with what you can really afford? Does it match up with meeting your goals?

It was 1999 and the entire IT department was working overtime sorting out over 5 million lines of code for the upcoming Y2K problem. Steve Taylor had just been promoted to manage his own sales team after eight years as a senior sales associate.

He wasn't nervous about the promotion. What did cause him to lose a bit of sleep at night were the IT department's ominous warnings about Y2K and its potential harm to the company—and to his paycheck.

"Bob, given what you know, what are the odds this will hurt our customers?" Steve asked the IT department head.

"If I knew—if any of us actually had an answer—we'd tell you Steve. Just prepare for a big dip in sales. Our com-

pany is playing catch-up, and I'm not sure how this is all going to affect us," Bob lamented.

Steve wasn't only worried about the company's future; his main concern was his family. His wife, Nancy, had just semi-retired from teaching and was enjoying raising their children. They had just purchased a new minivan and made a down payment to a contractor for another addition to their home. In their minds, the extra room was necessary. They had purchased a small home when they first got married. They added an additional bedroom when Sara, their third child was born. The new addition, a fourth bedroom, would not only make the house more livable, but sellable as well.

"It would be a good investment," he had thought to himself when making the decision about the addition.

Bob's discouraging words about Y2K, however, had put a wet blanket on Steve's hopes for a peaceful, prosperous New Year. He and Nancy believed the investment in the addition was like money in the bank.

"More like money TO the bank," he would later regret.

With the new payment on the van and the home addition, they were able to just get by on Steve's salary. He was banking on his overrides to put them well into the black. The kids needed a college fund, and he knew the best time to save was early and often.

Unfortunately, they had done neither.

Sound familiar?

For too many people, life tends to be a game of catch up. Even when we do get the bonus, windfall, or pay raise, we rarely see that as an opportunity to save more. Instead, we congratulate ourselves for our achievement with a purchase.

The simple fact that your income increased is no reason to increase your expenses right along with it. You're supposed to be *expanding* that buffer between income and expenses, not shrinking it. Going from making $50,000 a year to $100,000 a year does you absolutely no good if your annual expenses go from $40,000 a year to $95,000 a year. In such a case, you were better off with the lower income; at least then you knew how to budget.

The first step to financial wellness, then, is to examine your lifestyle. Otherwise all other efforts are doomed to failure. Develop some discipline, and stop trying to keep up with the Joneses, because guess what? They're broke, too.

It was now almost 2:30 a.m., and Steve Taylor was wide awake.

He had ordered a cup of tea about 30 minutes ago. As he stared, wide-eyed at the clock, the seconds of the night, like his life, ticked away without pause.

It was like watching a time bomb count down.

The nurse finally came in, but not with his cup of tea. She was wheeling in a new patient. A man at least 30 years older than Steve, his hair like snowy white drifts, with a smile that would remind anyone of his or her favorite uncle; all he needed was to be sitting on a porch swing with a glass of lemonade in his hand.

"Harold, you're terrible," the nurse was saying to the old man as they came in.

"My lil' filly, if I was ever the perfect gentleman, then I'd have never gotten to so many kids an' grandkids."

As the nurse wheeled him by, the old man flashed a smile and quick wink for Steve. With pale skin, slightly sunken and darkened eyes, Harold was obviously very sick. Yet, he still had a merry twinkle in his eye that seemed to make clear that the worst that life had to offer had slid off this guy like water off a duck's back.

Steve watched as the nurse helped Harold into the bed next to his own, finally drawing the covers up over him then folding the wheelchair up into a corner.

"Would you like me to draw the curtains around your bed, Harold?'

"Naw," the old man replied to the nurse's question. "That wouldn't be neighborly. I gots me a neighbor, and from the looks of him he could do with a bit of conversatin'. You jus' remember, that if it don't work out with that boyfriend of yours, I have next dibs."

"Don't worry," the nurse said with a broad smile. "I won't forget."

The nurse left the room, closing the door behind her, leaving just Steve and the old man alone in the room.

"Name's Harold. Of course, I'm guessing you got that by now."

The other man crumbled. "Steve. Steve Taylor."

"Well Steve, Steve Taylor, what all got you so glum?"

Steve just looked at the man in disbelief then weakly plopped his head back into his pillow with a tired sigh.

"Um, I'm going to die of liver cancer. It's kind of a glum topic, Harold. What about you? You seem like you are on some kind of happy drug?"

"Oh, I know that plenty fine, and I ain't on no drugs. Unless you call life a drug. Nope, my time is just about done, and eternity is just round the corner. I'm a believer, and I ain't afraid. In the next few days, my entire family will be by to see me off. Five kids, a dozen grandkids, and a wife who could still give that nurse some competition. I got about three different types of cancer and will be seeing the good Lord soon enough."

The way he said it caught Steve's immediate attention. The old man's prognosis of doom definitely did not jibe with his apparent happy mood. Steve turned his head on his pillow to face the old man, the question on his lips. He took a big pause and stared at Harold's deep, sunken, but twinkling eyes. "How can you be so happy?" Steve asked.

"You're sayin' I should be all glum like yourself? I suppose I could shout and cry, but the truth is that I've done everything I set out to do: My kids and grandkids are taken care of, and my wife will be sittin' pretty. Nope, nothin' to be sorrowful about."

"Fine when you're a millionaire with plenty of money to leave everyone."

"You think I'm rich? Boy, I just been a poor workin' stiff my entire life. Got nothin' special 'bout me that ain't no one else have."

"Then, how could you possibly have saved up enough to take care of five grown children and so many grandchildren? I've been slaving my entire life to keep my family fed and clothed, with little time to actually spend with them. And now, now I'll never get to—"

"Well, now that's your first mistake right there. You put money before family."

"I need money for *my family,"* Steve protested.

"An' who don't? But if you put money first, then actually spending time with your family will be the very last thing you ever get. Like my pappy used to say, you can't hug a wallet."

"Then how in the world was I ever to save up enough money for them all if I didn't work and slave?"

"Slavin's what got you into that bed you're on, son," the man grinned. *"But I'm guessin' you're missin' a couple of the basics."*

"I'm 48, ran a large division at my company. I learned the basics long ago."

"My son's about your age as well, and he still knows enough to listen to some good advice."

"Why? I'm about to die anyway."

"Boy, don't you know it's never too late? Now, you gonna listen?"

Steve relented with a sigh, after which Harold began his lecture.

"Now, you don't have to be pinchin' pennies like a miser to save a buck and live a good life. It's all about knowin' how to manage what you already have. To start with, always remember to pay yourself first..."

Managing Cash Flow

Managing your cash flow is the single greatest denominator of financial success, it is, as Harold put it, the "basics." It doesn't matter how much you make if you can't control how much goes out in terms of spending. The basics for managing your cash flow are pretty straightforward, so let me break it down into a few strategic points.

Automatic Savings Plans

"Pay yourself first" is not a new saying, but it's seldom one that's heeded. One of the reasons 401k programs are so popular is your money is saved before you even have a chance to spend it. 401k plans and IRAs from rolled over 401k plans make up at least 80 percent of most people's retirement savings.

Although I am proficient with financial planning, in the end I'm no different than most of you reading this book; I have a propensity for spending money when I see that bonus hit my checking account. One of my best solutions has always been to treat my investment accounts like bills— my most important bills. I tell people to save a minimum of 10 percent of their gross pay to be able to retire one day. Save 15 percent and retire early—and with style! Or save 20 percent and you will be the envy of your peers and, more importantly, have it truly made relative to your income.

I connect each of my investment accounts to a future goal: retirement, college for my kids, vacations, home improvements, and future weddings. I have money automatically taken out of my checking account every month to fund these important savings goals, *even before I've paid any of my other bills.*

The other bills (mortgage, utilities, etc.) always get paid. But, even if it is seconds or days later, the future "bills"—my long-term goals—are first in line.

That doesn't always leave a lot of money for discretionary spending. The last thing I need is a large credit card bill. This is why credit cards are such a very small part of my life, and a weekly allowance makes it all possible. If I see my checking account balance is running low, I *choose not to spend money on discretionary thing*s. That means not going out on the weekend, brown bagging it to work and eating leftovers, and saying "No" to my kids when they ask me for money. "You can't squeeze blood from a turnip."

We all work hard for our money. It's very rewarding to see our assets grow a little every month because of automatic savings programs. The financial peace of mind that comes from being on pace to fund my priority goals is the reason I use these automatic savings programs.

If it's possible that your goals are not funded the way you would like, I hope this guidance inspires you to make some changes. But, if you have trouble getting by with the money you earn today, then step one to improve your life beyond money is taking steps to save a portion of your next raise or bonus.

Is this a painful habit to form? Does it make you feel "cheap?"

No. It will make you feel very abundant. You simply have to reframe your thinking.

Control Your Discretionary Spending

Most people feel proud when they can pay off their monthly credit card payment in full. In fact, most of my clients tell me they seldom carry a balance from month to month, so it comes as a big surprise when I tell them, "Even if you pay off your credit card bill in full each month, you are probably hiding a rather large spending problem you're not aware of."

Your problem is not the pay off. It's the spending.

After roughly 30 years in the financial planning business, my unscientific studies have shown that 20 to 30 percent of your credit card purchases are made on very "marginal" items as defined by you. These are things you could easily do without, and most of these purchases were probably impulse buys. Imagine if you still had that money and could have invested it somewhere instead. How much would you have gained? A good rule of thumb to tell if a purchase wasn't all that important is if you can't recall what you spent the money on. Now add up the amount you spent on such forgotten purchases. How much money did you lose? How much could you have if you'd saved it instead?

My goal is to help you stop making those marginal buys and instead automatically funnel more of your money into investment accounts that are better aligned with your *real* priorities.

Discretionary spending is usually the area that gives people the most trouble. It's difficult to simply say "No" to the many little items that pass in front of our eyes all day long. But one way to change your monthly spending and get serious about improving your financial situation is to stop using credit cards. Period. Try keeping just *one* for gas, travel, and *real* emergencies (like a medical emergency, or your car broke down somewhere around Barstow), but tear the other ones up; go cold turkey. Otherwise stick with using cash.

"Credit cards?" the old man said with raised eyebrow. "Boy, I tore up all but one of my credit cards decades ago."

"But what if there's something you really need to get?" Steve asked. "What do you do then?"

The old man just looked at him and shook his head.

"Son, if I can't buy it with what's in my pocket at the time, then it's not something that I really need. Why, if I thought your way I'd be the proud owner of about 50 knickknacks to put on a fireplace mantel I ain't got. They'd just be lyin' in a corner gatherin' dust along with a Captain Spaceman decoder ring that

seemed like a good idea at the time. Now, there was that one time I was stuck halfway to Fresno when my car broke down, but that's when I finally had to break out my ATM card. That's what you call a real *emergency, not impulse buying some new do everything tech gadget like an Apple Watch."*

"But, how do you resist the temptation? I'll admit that my wife is not the only one who makes impulse buys."

"Really simple, boy. Pretend you're nine and your pappy's givin' you an allowance, only you're the pappy givin' yourself an allowance. Then ask yourself–and be honest now: Is this something that I'm gonna care about in 24 hours? A week? If not, then maybe you should be rethinking that purchase. Me, I just keep the same set amount of cash in my pocket every week, an' if I'm about to go over it, then it's time to just grit my teeth and wait until the next week."

Brad's Old School Cash Allowance System

I was once a single 20-something making pretty good money and living it up in Lincoln Park, Chicago. I'd go out frequently and spend most of my money on food and entertainment. The ATM was at a 7/11 a block from my apartment, and I was on a first name basis with all the cashiers. Then one day my less-than-thrifty ways smacked me straight in the face when my parents asked me a simple question. They asked me how much money I'd saved in the past year. The answer was next to nothing.

Given that I was a finance major in college and working in that field, the answer left me feeling ashamed. That shame motivated me to make the most important change I have ever made regarding my finances: I started living on a self-imposed fixed amount of weekly cash. I remember giving myself $300 a week for all my discretionary spending, which was a lot less than I had been blowing. At the same time, I set up a $500 per month automatic savings plan.

Living with a fixed amount of cash in my wallet was a real game changer. It changed my life. I started caring about everything I bought, as I realized those little things really add up. Just making my own 20 oz. coffee in a to-go cup saved me $20 per week (that's $1,000 a year!). Instead of eating out with my co-workers four days a week, I would grab a $4 salad at Jewel, saving me $40 per week ($2,000 a year!). Since I usually didn't have much money in my wallet and no credit card, I no longer bought late night drinks at the local watering hole. That surely saved me a pretty penny.

I did make sure to have money for what my priorities were at that point of my life: A Friday and Saturday round of golf, one Happy Hour a week, and a good weekend dinner to go along with plenty of pizza during the week.

I've shared my cash allowance system with many of my clients struggling to save money, and it comes down to a basic enough concept: If there's not enough cash in your pocket, then don't buy it. It's that simple. Decide on a reasonable amount you'll need for a week's worth of out-of-pocket expenses (including groceries), then make sure that's what you have in your pocket for a given week and no more. If you run out before the week's up, that means you'll have to budget more carefully next week, but right now you're out of luck. You may be asking why you should bother to do this. Why should you tear up your credit card and live on an allowance like a child? Let's look at a few reasons:

- You have ongoing credit card debt.
- Your emergency fund is nearly nonexistent.
- You don't have nearly enough money saved up for retirement.
- You don't have much saved to help your kids pay for college.

I could go on.

"I'll admit, there was a time when my wife would be drawn into anyplace with a 'Sale' sign attached to it. Said she was savin' money by buyin' it on sale, until of course we figured out that we'd save even more money by not buyin' it at all."

"My wife's a great mother, but she and I are both a bit of a shopaholic when it comes to our kids," Steve admitted. "I'm probably going broke because of it."

"There's a few ways around that. I finally put my foot down and started with a pad of paper and a pen."

"Paper and pen?"

"For the list," Harold grinned. "If it ain't on the list, ya' don't get it. And no fair bringin' the pen with you to keep adding to the list as you go."

"That's not a bad idea. But our monthly expenses are probably more than they were in your day. Cell phones, cable TV, lawn maintenance, are all things your generation proba…"

Harold cut Steve off.

"What in tarnation you need lawn maintenance for? That's why you got kids. Each of my sons had his turn at the lawnmower; taught them responsibility. Why, one of them even turned it into a weekend business. Didn't get much more'n 10 bucks a month, but when you're 12 that's a lot of money. He learned the basics of running a business, and now he's got one of his own and doin' pretty good for himself."

Steve turned the idea over in his head for a bit then gave a reluctant nod.

"You know, I remember how my dad used to have me mow the lawn every Saturday. I'd turn it into a game, racing the lawnmower up and down the yard until I got stuck by a particularly dense clump of weeds. I didn't always like it, but I did it."

"Your pappy sounds like he was a wise man," Harold nodded.

"Okay," Steve shrugged. "What else you got?"

"Well," Harold turned the thought around in his head for a bit before replying. "I got some tips on shoppin', if you wanna listen to them."

"Oh, my wife cuts coupons all the time and hits all the sales at the local Food Buster."

"And in that one sentence you've mentioned a whole buncha stuff that you do wrong," the old man chuckled. "For one thing, I *know Food Buster, and their sale prices don't amount to a hoot and a holler compared to the* regular *prices over at a couple other stores I know of. Here, you takin' notes on this? Because I got me a mess of tips that it sounds like you really need to hear."*

Easy Shopping Tips

Here are a few tips to managing your monthly cash flow. They're just simple little alterations to your lifestyle, but as we have seen, little things add up:

- Shopping is not the way to spend your free time. Take a walk in the park instead. My wife tells me that some days she doesn't leave the house for fear of being tempted to shop.

- Ideally, shop with a list. Plan out your week's meals ahead of time, based on your budget, then buy only what you need for those meals. Not on the list? Then not this week.

- Minimize drink orders at a restaurant. Try water, or something like an iced tea if you must, but stay away from the over-priced alcohol. Restaurants make most of their profit margin on drink orders. If you want to teach your kids a lesson when they keep insisting on getting some overpriced mega-sized soda, simply tell them to pay for their own drinks. *Then* you'll see how much they really want it.

- No more impulse buying. I don't care if it's on sale, or a "great" online deal; it's always expensive if it's something that you don't need. Wait a few days, then see if

16

you really need it. After all, do you really need *another* pair of shoes?

- Ignore the "bonus points" or miles your credit card (the only one you've kept!) gets you. You'll save a lot more money by not spending the money in the first place.

- Learn to ignore the word "SALE;" it's like a voodoo spell for some people. It doesn't matter if it's something you've never ever had a use for, people see that one word and rush in to buy the sale item. "Hey, there's a sale on tweezers; let's get a pair!" If you see that word "SALE," just keep on driving.

- If you're a real shopaholic, then try leaving the money in the car. Take into a store only what you need to buy what you came there for. This should help eliminate impulse buying.

- Don't fall for the sales pitch. New and shiny does not equate to being an actual *need*. Your car has 100,000 miles on it, but does it still work as well as it always has? Yes? Then why replace it with some new expensive gas-guzzler when you're trying to save up for your kids' college fund?

- Do you *really* need to eat out that much if your wife is a good cook and willing to put out the candles for date night? My wife is a good cook, plus we brew our own coffee, so that's two bonus points.

- Finally, learn to do things yourself. Your front yard consists of a measly 200 square feet of grass and one fruit tree, so why are you hiring gardeners? Stick a lawnmower in your son's hands, and break out the pruning shears for yourself. Are there other simple little things that you can manage on your own without calling "the guy?"

Of course, with kids you have a battle ahead of you. Try convincing them that for the price of a Blizzard from Dairy Queen they could get a whole gallon of ice cream at Walmart.

"I guess some of that sort of makes sense."

"Boy, it all makes sense. Why, we gave up treating our kids to the local Dairy Queen long ago; instead, every other Saturday we'd just get a gallon of ice cream, and my wife would show them how to make homemade sundaes. Turned it into a fun little contest and saved a bundle of money in the process."

"But it's all… Well, just too simple."

"Oh, you're one of those that expect all solutions have to be complicated an' involve some nine-point-plan that only a revenuer could understand. Son, sometimes the answer is as simple as it seems."

Lying there listening to the old man explaining things to him in the middle of the night, with nothing but the quiet drone of the air conditioner as competition, Steve was starting to believe that just maybe it really was all that simple. But there was still one thing that pestered him.

"Well, okay, so some of that I guess I can manage. But it's different when you're married."

"Do you love her?"

"Yes, of course."

"Then there's no reason to let a little money get between you. Savin' up's no different when you're a couple; you jus' have to make a few little adjustments. I'm just lucky I didn't marry no spendthrift wastrel."

Money and Marriage

The majority of marital problems stem from bad finances and arguments over spending. This is why being on the same page as your spouse when it comes to finances is absolutely *critical* to a happy marriage. You have to ensure that your priorities have some common ground. You might see a pressing need for that new big screen TV, but she'll remind you that without a new washer/dryer, that weekly flood of water in the laundry room is not going to get any better. The budget can only afford one or the other, so it's times like this when you need to be in synch.

I got lucky when I found a woman even more frugal than I am. I grew up with a mother who shopped with a grocery list and sewed patches onto my jeans whenever I tore them. My wife, meanwhile, grew up as one of eight children in a household where her father died when she was eight-years-old. Her mother ran a tight ship to raise those children under those circumstances. Luckily, my wife brought her frugal habits to our marriage. It's pretty easy, then, for the two of us to find

19

common ground on financial situations. If you and your spouse seem to have trouble finding common ground on financial decisions, then I suggest you look into how your spouse grew up and how that has influenced him or her.

Imagine, though, if I had married someone with quite a different upbringing. Suppose I'd married someone who was given a car for her sixteenth birthday. Or as a teenager never had to work for a buck or even help out around the house. Imagine if she was given her parents' credit card when she went to the mall. Or no chores since the gardeners did all the work. Where her mother caved into every child's impulse while walking down the grocery aisle. We'd be butting heads and either bankrupt or divorced. Probably both.

Being on the same page with your spouse regarding spending habits will not only be good for your savings, but good for the marriage as well. This is especially true when you have kids. Kids are expensive under the best of circumstances. But when you start trying to keep up with how cute the other toddlers in the neighborhood look, or every child's whim as your kid gets older instead of what the household actually needs, then you're never going to get anything saved up in that retirement fund.

Full disclosure: I admit to struggling with this and losing the battle many times.

Vacationing with my family is at the top of my life's priority list. I save for it every year, but I need to look for ways to manage the costs. Plane trips for a large family can get very expensive, so consider taking a road trip. Pile all your kids into the minivan, and give them a memorable scenic tour on the way over. Even if you can afford a plane trip, this will teach them a bit of humility and how to make do with what they have.

I have found that when the non-working spouse is the one charged with paying the bills then he or she runs a pretty tight financial ship. One of the best tips from *The Millionaire Next Door* is to marry someone more frugal then you; I agree whole-heartedly with that one. At the very least, if you have a problem financially then don't be afraid to discuss it with your spouse.

Budgeting can bring the two of you closer together as a team as well as a couple and provide you with the means to save both your marriage and your financial future.

"Back when my three older kids were somethin' like eight, nine, and ten, I came up with a dandy way to save on a trip and have fun at the same time."

"Then please do tell," Steve said, leaning forward with a bit of interest, "because I'm always going broke every time the word 'vacation' even comes up."

"Okay," the old man began. "We were going to spend a spring vacation in San Diego, and I brought twelve-hundred bucks in cash with me. Well, our first family meal was breakfast, and when we played 'guess the bill' nobody was even close to guessing the 85 dollars, and that was before the tip. It didn't take no financial planner to know that something had to change or I was going to run out halfway through the trip."

"*That happened to me once,*" Steve nodded. "*What'd you do?*"

"*First off, we grabbed a bunch of snacks from a nearby Walmart. Then I took a flyer and decided to give each of my three kids 30 bucks in cash. They were so happy to get that unexpected gift that they didn't seem to mind the strings attached. They could spend that money any way they wanted, but were not to ask me or their mother for no treats or trinkets, and if they wanted a drink—other than with dinner—it had to come out of their money. They were all in for it.*"

"*You must have saved a bundle with that trick,*" Steve chuckled.

"*Oh, you bet I did. Even better, though, is they started to learn about handling their own finances. They shopped and looked for deals, set their own priorities, the whole bit. I kept up that tradition, raising the amount over time, and I must say that my kids grew up to be pretty good with their money because of it. Later on, they each did it with their own kids.*"

"*Too bad that kind of trick can't work with my wife and me,*" Steve sighed. "*Trying to tell her how to spend her money is just asking for it.*"

Here Harold again smiled, a sign that Steve was coming to learn meant that there was something he was missing. Steve just shot him a glance, to which Harold replied.

"*It all just depends on how you go about it, son. Couples can have their own cash allowance system same as anybody else.*"

The Cash Allowance System for Couples

Harking back to my cash allowance system for a bit, this is an excellent exercise for married couples. Obviously, men and women have different priorities regarding what's important to spend money on, and when cash is short, finger pointing and blame can create serious trouble in a marriage. As many of you know, finances are at the top of the marital argument list, so we want to minimize this at all costs. If you try the cash allowance system that I've used for years, make sure you and your spouse have a sufficient amount each week. By using this system, you have decided to control your discretionary spending by fixing your discretionary spending *money*.

Adults don't want to be told how they can spend their money or what they can buy. But the reality is that you will prioritize due to the fixed amount of money you have so as to always have enough. As long as your spouse doesn't come asking for more money, you shouldn't have to worry how they spend their share. You should also create a couple "fun money" allowance in a separate envelope. First, it will hopefully remind you to go out and have fun together, but at the same time you won't have to worry about whose allowance that money should come from. I can almost guarantee that if you try this, giving both spouses a hefty weekly cash allowance, you still will be spending far less than what you used to spend with credit cards!

23

———————— ⌇ ————————

"So, changing my lifestyle is the first step to getting control of my finances."

"Jus' like a patient in this here hospital, son. You have to make sure they're stable before you can operate."

"Sort of like... financial wellness."

"There you go," Harold smiled. "Once you have that done, then you can go on to the next step."

"Saving money?"

"Now see? That weren't hard to figure out. People like you and me who aren't born rich or somethin' jus' gotta face all sorts of pressures an' worry when your financial health's not in order. That's why you're so glum, and I'm ready to check out and see what comes after."

"All this financial stress has been putting a burden on my relationship with my wife, and then with the costs for my health-care and—"

"Now ease up there, let's just go a step at a time. Now ya' know, I've known plenty of people who earn all sorts of big money, but you know what? They're not happy either, because they's got their own money worries. It's all relative, as they say. You jus' gotta remember that money is like fuel in your gas tank; it's neither the destination nor the vehicle. The goal's not money, boy, it's happiness."

24

Highlights

- Managing your monthly cash flow is critical to financial success.

- Paying yourself first is about the most important financial decision you can ever make.

- If you pay yourself first (ideally save 20 percent of your income) and don't go into credit card debt, you are doing well.

- I tell people to save a minimum of 10 percent of their gross pay to be able to retire one day. Save 15 percent and retire early and with style. Save 20 percent, and you will be the envy of your peers and, more importantly, have it truly made relative to your income.

- Affordable credit card purchases on marginal items quietly steal wealth and prevent you from being as financially successful as you could be.

- Discretionary spending should ideally be done with cash or a fixed amount of money.

- Brad's Old School Cash Allowance System is a solution for curbing discretionary spending:

  - Strive to understand how your spouse values money.

  - Create joint goals based on your joint priorities, and use your priorities as a compass for your automatic savings plans—your life goals are your motivation to save.

  $\longrightarrow$

- Communication is critical in any marriage—curb discretionary spending by agreeing on cash allowances if you can't find money to save.

- Budgets make us better parents. You don't want to spend too little on your kids, but you could also spend too much on them. You want them to grow up to be responsible self-sufficient human beings, not spoiled, entitled drains on society. Budgeting allows you to set aside appropriate levels of funding for education, clothing, sports, music, and fun.

~ Chapter Two ~

Saving

"A penny saved is a penny earned."

Your savings habits have a very big impact on your financial wellness, but the problem with a lot of couples is that they do not seem to know the meaning of the words "saving money". A lot of people have a tendency to live to the very limit of their means, getting their credit cards paid off on time every month but leaving nothing left to add to their savings. This can be really bad for a number of reasons. To name a few:

- An emergency comes up, such as your car breaking down, but you only have $500 in your savings. So *now* what?
- What about your kids' college fund?
- Planning to retire in style? You won't if you don't have six or seven figures saved up.

So, let's look over what some extra savings can get you and some little tricks to get there. One obvious question that always comes up: When is the best time to start saving? The answer is much like what the gardener will tell you when the best time to plant a tree is, either 10 years ago or right now.

"Okay, first question," Harold began. "Do you at least have your emergency fund?"

The puzzled expression on Steve's face said it all as he stammered out a reply.

"My emergency—Well, we've been too busy trying to make ends meet, and, besides, we never figured that—"

"Son," Harold sighed, "unless you been blessed by the Almighty himself, you will have an emergency. An' when you do, you best be ready for it. Cus' iff'n you ain't, then that emergency money has got to come outta somewhere, and I'm betting it's not going to be somewhere pleasant."

Your Emergency Fund

Survey: How much money do you have saved in your saving account?

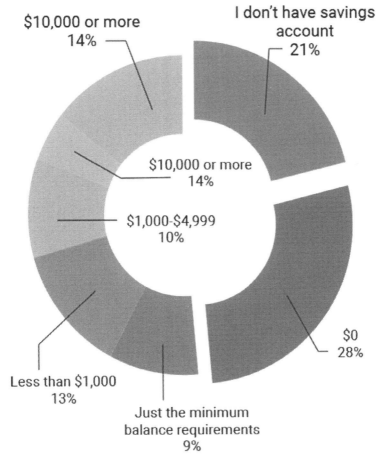

$10,000 or more
14%

I don't have savings account
21%

$10,000 or more
14%

$1,000-$4,999
10%

$0
28%

Less than $1,000
13%

Just the minimum balance requirements
9%

Source: GOBankingRates.com

RK Financial Wellness

The foundation of your financial pyramid is a large pile of cash readily available. It may not be earning much sitting there in your normal savings account (less than 1 percent nowadays), but having it around will head off a number of headaches for life's little surprises. Now, I'm not just talking a few hundred to a couple thousand dollars, but more on the order of ten to twenty thousand or more. Of course, the exact amount will be dependent on your income and how much you can squirrel away, but this is more in the range I'm talking about.

The reason? Well, there are reasons why it's called an *emergency* fund. Just in one year I've seen one of my clients need a new furnace for $2,400, another plan a surprise vacation for $7,500, one couple handle their daughter's marriage for $30,000, while another bought a new Winnebago at $70,000 for their retirement. Then of course there's the question of what might happen if you lose your job; how long could you survive on what's in your savings right *now*?

Like I said, a large pile of cash is the basis for any solid financial plan. With it, you can not only deal with emergencies without too much panic, but also handle a few other things, such as:

- Taking advantage of sales on non-durable goods
- Travel—weekend getaways or major family vacations
- Home improvements
- Gifts
- Fewer worries if investment values decline when you're not depending on using that money in the near term

- Keeping higher insurance deductibles when your cash allows you to self-insure, thus saving you on the premium
- Never having to worry about credit card debt

Need I say more?

Okay, so having that extra cash lying around is a really good thing, but how do you get it there in the first place? And how does one get some money saved up for other funds like college or retirement? That's our next thing to look at.

Harold was in the bed nearest the window, the moonlight lazily drifting in, illuminating him in a soft glow as he spoke. Steve had been listening to every word the old man had said, but still couldn't help but shake his head.

"But, how am I ever supposed to save anything up? It seems that as soon as I get a paycheck, it's already been spent."

"Then," the man said with a mischievous gleam in his eyes, "jus' make sure that you don't get the money in the first place. At least not all of it."

"Huh? Is this some sort of old Southern trickery?"

"Not at all. Jus' a little of that head-shrinkin' stuff."

"Psychology?"

"That's the word," Harold nodded. "Now listen close. It's a bit like takin' the eggs out of the hen house before the chicken-hawk even realizes they're there..."

31

Automatic Savings Transfer

The problem with a lot of people is that they have an affluent lifestyle but very little money saved compared to what they've earned. Just because they might have some money left over after the bills seems to mean they have to go out and spend it all. But that simply isn't so. That's no way to increase your stockpile of cash, much less do anything about any of your other accounts (retirement, college for the kids, emergency fund, etc.).

For example, take this likely scene from a typical couple; let's call them Peg and Al.

Peg: Honey, do we have any money left this month?

Al: Just barely. I got all the bills paid, mortgage up-to-date, the children's expenses factored in. I think I have about 500 bucks left.

Peg: Oh, good. That means I can buy that new dress, and then you and I can go out tomorrow. We haven't been on a date in *so* long.

Al: But we need to save that. What if something comes up? And what about the kids' college fund?

Peg: Oh, there'll be plenty from next month's check we can save. Come on—or don't you love me anymore?

Al: Sigh…

There's nothing Al can do because the cash *is* there, and he wants to keep up a good relationship with his wife. What's he to do? How is he ever going to start stockpiling some extra cash if something like the above is a typical monthly scene?

The solution is simple. Just set up an automatic transfer from your checking account to your goal-related account(s). Make it automatic so you won't have to worry about forgetting to do it or any lack of discipline on your part. Set up the other account(s) that the money is being transferred to in a completely separate institution, away from where your checking and regular savings accounts are located. That way there won't be the temptation to cheat a little. If the branch of the other place is on the other side of town, then even better, as you'd be less likely to drive that much out of your way to cheat than if all you had to do was walk across the street. Your money is transferred to a completely separate account that you cannot easily get to, all nice and automatically.

Side benefit: Since this *does* happen automatically every month, you'll be seeing a lower amount of cash in your checking account than otherwise, which means you probably won't be wanting to spend as much on your credit card because you won't see as much available to pay it off with. Happy days!

Now suppose that Al and Peg have done this, and before Al even gets to write the bills every month it happens. The previous scene then reduces to the following:

Peg: Honey, do we have any money left this month?

Al (looking at what's left *after* the automatic transfer): Nope.

Peg: Okay.

With this auto-transfer in place, there are a few places that you can aim this transfer of funds towards. For instance:

- Long-term savings or emergency funds
- 529 college savings plan
- 401k plan increases
- Taxable brokerage account

This is also a good way to set aside funds for those all-important family vacation trips. I have two trips with my family every year, one at Easter and the other at Christmas, and while they are expensive, I wouldn't trade the experiences for anything. You can take this from your emergency fund or even create a separate vacation fund, if you're up to it.

Now let's look into a few tricks for saving some extra money to have for these accounts in the first place.

"Why, I was doin' this before computer automation even came around. Of course, back then it amounted to me doin' a bit of legwork at the bank every time I got a check. Had to race to make the deposits before my wife could think up something else to spend it on," Harold chuckled. "But it got all my kids through college and gave us a nice little nest egg."

"Okay, so that sounds like a good idea," Steve admitted. "But even with that in place, there just seems to be so many things; all these bills that keep adding up. Do you have any tips for that?"

The dead of night, dawn a couple hours away, his own death possibly not much further along than that, and here he was listening to some old man about how to plan for his future. Steve couldn't help but wonder at his own mistimed foolishness; per-

haps if he'd bumped into the old codger about 20 years ago... Still, he might as well hear the guy out.

"Boy, I got more tips for cuttin' corners than a raccoon has teeth. You jus' listen up and start takin' notes..."

Tips for Saving

There are a number of things, big and small, that you can do to save a little extra money every month. It doesn't involve getting a second job or robbing a bank, but simply looking at where you can shave a little bit of fat from your existing bills.

1) Set up and follow a weekly allowance

Okay, so I mentioned this in the last chapter, but it's important enough to be mentioned again. Imposing a weekly allowance on yourself is both a lifestyle change and a savings tip, so it belongs in both chapters and is worth stating again. Set yourself that weekly cash allowance; when you run out, then you'll just have to budget better next week.

2) Pay off that mortgage fast

Want to know what's even better than investing in a savings bond? Getting that mortgage paid off ASAP before the interest kills you. The faster you pay it off, the more extra money you'll have every month. I used to have a regular 30-year long-term loan on our home, then decided to refinance, and I changed it to a 15-year mortgage; my monthly payment was increased, but it gets the debt paid down that much faster. My wife and I can now look forward to owning our home free and clear quite a lot sooner, and then freeing up that extra money for other needs, such as our kids' college fund or our retirement accounts.

Think of it this way: After those first 15 years, you will have an extra couple thousand dollars a month that you won't be shelling out as compared to if you were still paying off on the 30-year plan.

Nowadays mortgages' terms are more flexible. I suggest you consider matching your mortgage payoff year with the year you hope to retire. For example, if you're 47-years-old and plan to retire at age 67 (when you qualify for full social security benefits) take out a 20-year mortgage rather than a 30 year.

3) Budget your bills

This can be a big one. Most people take their monthly bills for granted. You pay the internet, phone, and cable TV bills without looking and never bother to rate-compare any other service you might have a choice in.

Start with your cable TV. I did this a few years ago when it began to look like a little too much. Since I was getting Netflix, I dropped some movie channels and saved $25 a month. I could have gone for even more, but I just gotta have me some University of Iowa (my *alma mater*) sporting events from the B10 Network. You may have other things you wouldn't mind giving up, though, so examine your channel list, and then call your cable or satellite provider for a nice little chat.

Next is that cell phone bill. I have three teenagers in the house, which means that before I made changes we were always going over our data limit every month. With every extra gigabyte of data costing me another $15, I decided it was worth looking into an unlimited plan. Ten minutes on the AT&T live chat line later, and I'd cut $80 from my monthly cell phone bill. That's quite a notable chunk!

Then there's the internet bill. I'd been using Comcast until I realized there are other providers out there. A bit of shopping around, and I cut my internet from $65 a month to $55.

Don't forget those bundles you hear about. Get the phone, TV, and internet all in one nice tidy little package at a discount. But beware, and double-check to see if you really *would* be saving money overall with bundled services versus setting up two or all three of these with different companies. Maybe that cell phone provider you like so much really does have a low enough rate that it's still not worth it to go with the package deal from AT&T; or maybe you *did* find a bundle that could save you a bundle. You'll just have to start comparing.

In the end, though, it's worth the effort to shop around. Just with the phone, internet, and TV, I ended up saving $1,380 a year by looking around! Here's the breakdown of what I saved:

DirecTV: $25/month, or $300/year

Cell phone: $80/month, or $960/year

Home internet: $10/month, or $120/year

Total: $115/month, or $1,380 every year!

By the way, if I invested that $115 monthly savings for 20 years at 8 percent, I'd have an extra $67,000 in my pocket! If I did this for 30 years, it would be worth about $171,000! Now that's *real* money!

You may also have other services that you can shop around and save with. Of course, there are some, such as your basic gas and electricity, that your kind of stuck with, but you may have others that you can trim a little. Examine each of your services and monthly bills to see what can be removed or trimmed.

Car and house insurance, for instance—that's another good one to shop around, especially now with more companies having reduced rates if you carry both your car and house insurance with the same carrier. Talk with your insurance broker to check if you might be over-insuring something, or take advantage of the different types of discounts they might offer. In fact, the subject of insurance is so important that I'm going to cover it in more detail in the next chapter.

4) Learn when to say no to your kids

If you have kids, then you know what I'm about to say. Beyond the necessities of clothing and food, the minute they're old enough to start biking out to their friend's house or the local store, they're old enough to start holding out their hand for some extra cash. It could be for eating with their friends, getting comic books or other hobby-related goodies, or buying extra clothes not because they need them but because of the latest fad style. Before you can say, "My kid is never going to learn to be self-sufficient," you've already stuffed a few bills into their waiting hands just to shut them up.

Well, that's got to stop. See what they can do on their own, how much they can save, or how far they can stretch a buck. Even if you have the money, you're there to teach them some self-reliance, not to act as an ATM. Particularly in their teens when their monetary requests are only going to grow (a lot), you've got to stop spoiling them rotten. Your pocket book will like it, and their future selves will appreciate it.

So, the next time your kid holds out a hand, consider simply shaking it instead of filling it.

5) Save on your home purchase and add $1,000,000 to your retirement savings!

One significant source of saving money is in the home you buy. Most people don't take the big picture view when they take the plunge. They are driven more by their ego; the bigger, more expensive the home they own, the more successful people will know them to be.

Or maybe you're a first-time home owner and are blinded by the thrill of owning your very first home. You buy what you think will be your "dream home" early in life, but your emotions are blinding you to the unwise choice being made. You ask a mortgage lender or a realtor for advice, or maybe use an online calculator to figure out how much you can afford, but in reality, that's your first big mistake.

Using that monthly affordability number will set your sights on a home and mortgage that is way more expensive than what is in your ultimate financial interest. Those "affordability" assumptions can break you in the long-term.

For starters, those numbers will often be based on two incomes if both spouses are gainfully employed, which doesn't leave much flexibility if someone decides on a career change. Start a family, and the financial and home-related pressures skyrocket; either one spouse has to cut back or stop working, or the couple has to pay for daycare. Many couples fail to factor this in when they decide how expensive a home they can afford.

Many couples think that daycare will be their solution *before* they have their first child. Yet every parent knows their heart grows ten-fold when they have their first baby. The love and attachment sometimes grows to the point where a parent wants to stay home with their baby, but if they bought their first home based on their joint income, then this could add serious financial and marital stress to their relationship. This problem could have been avoided if they'd only thought ahead when they bought their house.

This is why buying based on *one* income—and an amount significantly less than the affordability numbers a mortgage lender allows—makes much greater financial sense to me.

Some people look at a home as an investment, but buying a home creates liabilities. Even if it sells for more than you paid for it, after you factor in all the annual expenses it creates, it's more often a financial loser than winner. It becomes an asset that may cost you thousands of dollars more than what you eventually sell it for. The true return you get for home owner-ship comes in less than quantifiable terms: the family memo-ries, the neighborhood, schools, friends, and so forth.

What sense does it make, then, to upset that unquantifi-able personal investment by finding yourself slipping into debt because you bought a far bigger home than you actually need?

Let's look at an example:

If you bought a $500,000 home in Glen Ellyn, Illinois in 2005, your home may be worth $600,000 today, and you could still be paying about $10,000 per year in property tax. After 13 years, that's $130,000 just in property taxes with little appreci-ation to make up for it, and that's not even counting all those home maintenance expenses you had to pay for. This is not to say that you shouldn't buy a cute home to enjoy, but rather, buy well under your means to ensure that you have some buffer for the future.

Let's look at some of the pre-retirement benefits of buying well under the lender affordability guidelines:

- Career flexibility:
  - One of you could stop working if he or she wants to be home more
  - You would be free to change jobs, even take a lower paying position that might make you happier
- Lower property taxes on a less expensive home
- Less pressure to keep up with the Joneses on things like how you furnish your home, the price of the cars you drive, landscaping costs, the preschools you send your

kids to, and the clothes and other things you are expected to buy for your children. (If you have kids, you know what I mean!) Remember, a higher-priced home begets higher-priced upkeep.

- More discretionary money—not "house poor":
  - Money for vacations
  - More money to save for retirement or college, or whatever you want in life.
  - You won't have to keep working well past retirement age just to pay everything off.

Imagine if you bought your first home at age 30 and instead of taking out a $300,000 mortgage, you bought a less expensive home and took out a $200,000 mortgage. This could save you $500 a month (in lower mortgage payments), which you could invest for the future. Investing $500 every month, earning an 8 percent annual return would grow to $750,000 in 30 years, $1,000,000 if you also count in the savings in property taxes.

Saving $500 every month earning 8 percent interest grows to $750,000 in 30 years, $1,000,000 when you include savings in property taxes!

Of course, you don't have to be a first-time buyer to make these mistakes; any time you buy a new house priced higher than you should be spending, the result could come back to bite you in the rear later in life. A high-priced home now could come into severe competition with your kids' college costs and your retirement fund later on.

If you did make the mistake of buying a really expensive home relative to your income, then one option at retirement is to downsize. Ideally, for many people it would be nice to have the option to retire in the same home where you made all those wonderful memories raising your family. Without a mortgage. And maybe even enough money saved up to travel, afford a vacation home, or whatever else you wouldn't be able to do had you decided on that more expensive home.

Of all the things you can do to save money, top of the list has to be not getting overzealous with that home purchase. A home purchase will impact your future career choices, your spending habits, your travel opportunities, your ability to save money, and it will cause you anxiety over your finances for the rest of your life. Once you make that big purchase, it won't be easy to go back.

"The point is to jus' look around. Examine every detail, and do your homework. I had my mortgage paid off just in time for my eldest to enter high school, which was great considerin' all the activities he started entering. Man, what his bein' in the school band cost me just in uniforms alone. Had another right behind him who wanted to enter band as well, just so the two of them could form their own trumpet section. Fortunately, without that mortgage hangin' over my head, I could also start puttin' some of that money towards their college years."

A smile crossed Harold's face as he reminisced over what were obviously fond memories. For himself, Steve could only sigh in regret.

"I don't have the time to look at every single aspect of my bills like that."

"Then make the time; unless you don't think savin' money is worth it. Why, I saved 30 bucks a month just shoppin' around phone plans. That's nearly 400 a year, son. You don't think that's worth it? Then once the kids were all in college I realized me and the wife didn't have much use for cable television, so I broke out an old pair of rabbit ears and started saving about five or six thousand a year."

Hearing numbers like that definitely got Steve's attention. He sat up straighter, his pillows at his back now, as he turned his full focus on what the old man was saying.

"I really could save me that much money?"

"I think you'd be surprised, son. How do you think I gave all my kids a future? It started with just findin' ways to be savin' money."

"I remember when we had our first kid," Steve sighed. "Happiest moment in my life."

"It usually is," Harold grinned. "So what'd you do first?"

"Well, we only had a little two-bedroom house and had been planning on building an addition. We figured then was the time."

"And how long were you paying for it?" Harold asked.

Steve's fond recollection turned quickly sour as he jerked the covers up closer to his chin.

"Too long," he grumbled. "It started an avalanche of debt we're still trying to get out from under. I just wish I'd waited a little longer. What'd you do when you had your first kid?"

"Well," Harold replied, "I was just a working stiff same as anyone else, but I did my homework and decided it best to start savin' up for the kid's college. The day after I found out that my wife was pregnant–once I got finished dancing her around the livin' room, of course–I put $100 into a college fund for the kid. Then, each month, an automatic transfer would put another hundred in, straight outta my paycheck."

"Wasn't it hard living without that hundred, though?"

"The way my wife clips coupons, son? She became the Coupon Queen of the County; we never noticed a thing. The little tyke didn't need much more'n crib-space for a while anyway, so I was able to hold off on our own little room addition until I had actual cash-money to deal with it. Which, considering how much I was scrimping away from budgeting and whatnot, was not all that much longer. The boy was about four before he and his little brother finally got a room of their own. I did my own yard work, took a bicycle to the neighborhood grocery store instead of wastin' gas driving, and jus' cut out cable television entirely–I mean, what does a toddler need cable for anyway? Oh, we got cable TV back in time for the kid to start enjoying the good cartoons the way he should, but even then, we found a really good deal."

"Okay, so I get it," Steve said with a tired sigh. "Then what's next?"

Harold reached over to pick up a glass of water the nurse had left for him on his nightstand, taking a sip before continuing.

"Next is one of them big words that most folk don't like usin'. That's why I had to get me a sip of water, so just' listen close 'cause I have just enough energy to get through this the one time."

The clock on the wall was just hitting 3:30 as Harold continued.

Highlights

- Having an emergency fund is the foundation of your financial pyramid.
- Set up an automatic savings transfer from your checking account to fund your long-term savings accounts.
- A few tips for saving money:
  - Set a weekly allowance.
  - Align your mortgage payoff with your expected retirement year.
  - Budget your bills.
- Buy well-under what the mortgage lenders will qualify you to borrow.
- Buy based on only one income if both spouses work.

~ Chapter Three ~

Insurance

"There are risks and costs to a program of action. But they are far less than the long-range risks and costs of comfortable inaction."
– John F. Kennedy

Insurance premiums can be a source of great expense, but there is also the need to provide for the future should a pressing situation arise. Be it car, health, or life, the purpose of insurance is to provide for an unexpected *emergency*—an unpredictable event of large financial magnitude. The size of your deductible should reflect this reality when weighed against the premiums you will be paying. Many people make the mistake of having too low of a deductible and including things that do not fall under the term "emergency." Smaller financial emergencies that could easily be covered out-of-pocket should not be covered by insurance, because it's usually not worth the higher premium cost. This is where that emergency fund of yours comes in handy; having a substantial emergency fund allows you to absorb smaller financial emergencies so that you can stomach a higher deductible to save money on premiums across the board. All a part of your personal financial symphony.

For example, that little fender bender you had in the parking lot—it cost you $400 to get it fixed, and reporting it would no doubt increase your premiums anyway, so why bother having a deductible any lower than $500 to begin with? Even for health insurance, you don't need to insure the expense of a basic checkup or doctor's visit for a common cold or flu, so why waste the money on a low deductible when the premium that you would have saved with a higher deductible could have easily paid for the bottle of aspirin you might need? Or for that matter a whole *shelf* of over-the-counter products.

So, let's look into insurance a bit deeper and see just how much you might need, where you can save some money on your premiums, and what are the critical types of insurance that you really *do* need.

"Insurance is too much of a complicated mess," Steve objected, "and too expensive."

"Well, don't cut it out completely," Harold chuckled, "otherwise it'll be like frog giggin' when you're a toad yourself; you cut off your own legs."

Steve had to admit that one was funny and grinned at the thought before continuing.

"But then, where do I start? I've seen so many different types of insurance plans, and confusing lingo, that I've just about had it."

"Well, I don't fault you on that one, Steve. Took me a bit of lookin' into to get the hang of how it all works myself, but I think I got it all boiled down now, if you're willing to listen to some old cuss too shot up with drugs?"

"Yeah, sorry about that. I've just been overwrought."

"Forgiven," Harold smiled. "If we was back at my old home then I'd be breakin' out some sweet tea right about now. Okay, insurance. Well, let's start with vehicle and house insurance."

"My rates are just killing me. Well, that and this liver."

"Hey, there you go," Harold beamed. "Humor. I'll make a southerner outta you yet. Well, when it comes to house and vehicle insurance, there's a few things I've learned over the years..."

Vehicle and House Insurance Basics

Of course, you want to make sure that your property is properly insured, but many people over-insure, resulting in needlessly higher premiums than they should be paying. This is where it pays to inspect every last little detail of your policies to see what you can live without. There are two general rules that you should be following at this point, and this goes for *any* type of insurance, be it car, house, life, or health:

1) The more the policy covers the higher your premiums will be.

2) The lower the deductible the higher the premium.

You want to ask yourself: Is the extra money I might save from a lower deductible for a *possible* claim worth the extra I *will* be paying every year on the premium? Unless you're in the habit of getting into a parking lot fender bender on a monthly basis, that $400 repair bill is easily covered out-of-pocket by what you'll save on the premium from *not* signing up for a deductible any lower than $500.

There was a survey completed a few years ago by InsuranceQuotes.com in which they wanted to find out how much the average consumer could save by raising their deductible. The results varied depending on demographics and where in the country one lives, but here's the thumbnail sketch of it all:

- If you raise your deductibles from $250 to $500, you can save 7 percent.
- If you raise your deductibles from $500 to $1000, you can save 9 percent.
- If you raise your deductibles from $500 to $2000 you can save 16 percent.

That could start to add up after a while, especially if you tend to go a long time between little fender benders. Sometimes out-of-pocket really is the cheaper way to go.

For house and property insurance, just how many things in your home do you *really* need to cover? One year my homeowner's insurance went up 13 percent from an across-the-board increase, so I looked into the details of my policy to see what I could trim. It turns out that there was a rider on the policy covering my wife's earrings, but they'd already been lost a few years earlier. We never filed the claim, and with a $1000 deductible it never made sense to pursue it. If I *had* filed a claim, then I would have lost the 15 percent, $225 per year, "no-claim" premium savings that I was enjoying. It wasn't worth filing a claim for, so keeping that coverage on there also wasn't worth it. We dropped that quickly.

The moral of the story? Watch what you insure; you may not need the coverage.

That same year I increased the deductible on my home insurance policy from $1000 to $2500, the reason being that if the house burns down then that extra $1500 won't amount to anything. But by just performing this one act—by increasing the main deductible from $1000 to $2500—I saved $375 per year on the premium payments! That difference paid for itself in just four years.

The same goes for cars. There are some options on your policy that only make sense for newer vehicles. If your car is, say, 10-years-old, then go over each item of coverage with your agent to see what's really worth keeping; you may not want collision coverage, for example.

It is worth the trouble every couple of years to analyze each of your policies to see if your coverage is up-to-date and if it's worth it to increase the deductible and save on your premium.

There are also a number of other ways to save on your premiums, in the form of "deductions." For vehicle insurance, you can get the list of fee deductions from your agent, but most of them will have multi-vehicle discounts (as much as 10 to 25 percent savings!), discounts for carrying both your vehicle and house insurance with the same carrier (around 10 to 20 percent on *both* policies), discounts for a good driving record (around 10 percent), discounts for low mileage (from about 2 to 10 percent), and even discounts for being in certain professions (yes, that science degree can save you money). Go through the policy options with a magnifying glass, and do not wait for your agent to suggest anything (he may not even be aware of all the finer options his company provides).

Let's go back to Al and Peg again. Suppose they have two vehicles and their house insurance. Insurance is $500 each for the vehicles and $1000 a year for the house. They have to pay out a total of $2000 a year for all this, so they start looking at ways to save some money and come up with this:

- Having two vehicles on the same carrier saves them 20 percent on car insurance.
- Having a multi-policy discount, meaning their car and house policies are both with the same carrier, saves them 20 percent on both car and house policies.
- Having a good driving record saves them 10 percent for the vehicles.
- Having generally low mileage saves them another 4 percent on car insurance.
- They qualify for a 3 percent Loyalty Discount (some carriers give this discount for sticking around a few years).
- Al is a shoe salesman so no discount for profession.

Added up, they get 57 percent saved off the two vehicles and 20 percent off the house insurance. Now they're paying $210 for each vehicle and $800 for the house insurance, for a total of $1220 per year on their insurance. That's quite a chunk of change they're saving.

Of course, when you start to look for ways to save, be sure that the essentials *are* covered. For a vehicle, this means watching out for that uninsured driver who's about to rear-end you by getting some uninsured and underinsured motorist coverage; I'd recommend at least $500,000 worth of coverage for this option. As they say, there are a lot of crazy drivers out there, and probably at least half of them do not carry enough insurance for the accidents they're about to cause.

For home insurance, this means fire for most homes, earthquake if you're in earthquake country (I'm looking at you, California), or even something for tornados if you live in the middle of Kansas. Take into account *where* you live and *how* you live. Do you drive a lot or a little? Is vandalism a frequent problem where you typically drive around? On the flip side of that, you probably do *not* need earthquake insurance if you *do* live in the middle of Kansas.

Compare what you know of your environment with what should be classified as "Required."

"Sure, I've had my share of fender benders. I think I average about one a decade. The worst one cost me about 400 bucks. Came straight outta my pocket."

"Your insurance didn't cover it?" Steve gasped.

"'Course not. Had my deductible set to $1,000. Saved me close to $800 a year that way. Over the 10 years I average between accidents, that's 8,000 bucks, son. You want I should pay out an extra 8,000 in insurance to cover a $400 repair? Pappy didn't raise no fool."

"I guess not... Wow, $8,000. I never thought of it in those terms before."

Just the thought of what he could do with that sort of money had Steve caught between wanting to cry and laugh. But Harold wasn't finished with him just yet.

"Then there's medical insurance."

"I got everything," Steve told him, "the full boat. It may be killing my pocketbook, but I want to make sure that my family is covered if something should happen."

"Then you're over-insuring yourself, son. Would you pay an extra 20 bucks a month just to insure against your kids getting a cold, or just break out a five-spot when you need to get a bottle of aspirin and a Band-Aid?"

"Well, I'd go for the fiver, of course. But what—"

"Then why in tarnation are you paying for all that extra insurance for something you can cover with what's in your wallet right now? Don't be a fool, boy. You don't need to insure your family against everything under the sun; just the big emergencies. Unless you want to make the insurance companies richer than they already are."

54

The old man had a point. Steve felt like a kid being scolded after caught doing something he should have known better than to do. In short, he felt embarrassed.

"Well, no. I guess that I just haven't thought things through like that."

"Then listen up, 'cause old Harold's learned a few tricks over the years…"

Medical Insurance

Medical insurance is another necessity that can get expensive if you don't engineer it right, but also one where you have to make sure you and your family have what you will need should something happen. It's a fine balance, but there are a few common mistakes that you can watch out for.

First, of course, is the same as for vehicle and home insurance: Don't go for too low a deductible. If a medical problem is something you can cover with a Band-Aid, a bottle of aspirin, or a basic doctor visit, then you can take that cost out of your pocket. Generally, you can go back to my three flags to tell you when you need insurance:

- Is it unpredictable?
- Is it unlikely to happen?
- Is it really expensive?

If you can say "Yes" to all three of these, then you're good to go with the insurance. But the flu, your annual checkup, or a teeth cleaning are not worth the extra premium getting covered for. In fact, there are a number of medical tests where the out-of-pocket fee would be as much as one-*tenth* what gets charged for those insured. Just look for clinics that offer "concierge" discounts. The chart below gives a comparison of some sample costs of hospital versus concierge rates. Quite a big difference; heck, even a colonoscopy gets down to $400 versus $2000.

Cost of Care

A sampling of tests and screenings offered by concierge clinics

Service	*Price charged by a lab, hospital or screening facility	**Concierge discount price
Prostate cancer (PSA) test	$175	$5
Thyroid (TSH levels) test	$94-$125	$10
Routine blood chemistry panel	$46 to $63	$15
Testosterone test	$227	$25
Vitamin D level test	$230	$25
X-Ray	$100	$30-$50
PAP smear	$92	$56
Mammogram	$350	$80
CAT scan	$500 per body part	$150-$470
MIRI brain (without contrast)	$600	$380
Colonoscopy	$2,000	$400

*A sampling of what patients pay-of-pocket, if the test isn't covered by insurance or if the deductible hasn't been met.

** What patient pay directly, without using insurance, Amounts can count toward deductible and out-of-pocket maximums.

How high *should* your deductibles be? Take a look at what sort of out-of-pocket costs you can handle for these and similar situations, then compare that to how much the higher deductible will save you on your premium from year to year. If there's a test you only need to take every three years that would cost $100 out-of-pocket, but save you $40 off your premium with the higher deductible, then go for it.

The main reason to go with a higher deductible is to save on your monthly premium. Ideally, if you go with a higher deductible, you would "bank" the premium savings so that when you have a claim, you would pay for it from the premium savings you put away. I guarantee that when you're on the hook for paying for more medical expenses, you will have incentive enough to shop around for the best price whenever possible. I have a $10,000 deductible for my family of five, and I promise you that I shop.

As a well-past-his-prime basketball player, I've had several X-rays and, more recently, MRIs in the past couple years. Rather than let my orthopedic get these done in his office, I shopped around and found a local imaging facility that does these for a fraction of the cost. Specifically, three X-rays of my knee for $45, and my knee MRI only cost me $300! This includes having a radiologist read both and then sending me an email the next day with the results.

One of the most important issues to review when you pick a policy is the doctor network. As a result of Obamacare, many insurers now only offer "skinny" hospital and doctor networks. Never assume your doctor will be in the network. The best way to check is to call the doctor's office directly *before* choosing your insurance plan and again before setting up your appointment.

You also want to make sure the policy covers the types of procedures you actually *want*. For instance, with dental insurance, if you ask a dentist, then he will tell you that certain types of fillings are not covered by insurance (basically those nice ceramic ones versus the standard gold filling); so, if this is the type of filling you'd be wanting to get for that nice, pretty smile, then you can leave that category of dental work out of your insurance policy and save some cash.

One very important part of the health insurance symphony is the Health Savings Account. In fact, having an HSA is *so* important that it merits its own section later on in this chapter.

Disability Income Insurance

The single most valuable asset you and your family have is income. After all, if something were to happen to you, how would your family survive without your income to provide for them? If you become disabled, it could spell disaster on your household income and financial plan if you are not properly insured. And News Flash: You are actually more likely to get disabled than die in your younger years.

There are two ways of getting disability insurance: on your own or through an employer.

Employer-provided disability insurance benefits make for a nice parachute should you become disabled, and are usually very inexpensive due to group-rates, but the benefits are restricted and not portable when you leave the company. If you do opt for an employer-provided insurance plan, there are a few things you have to remember:

1) The definition of disability: Most employer/group policies insure you in your own occupation for *only* two years. After that, they only pay the claim if you are unable to do any work that you could be trained to do. So, you'd have to be in very bad shape to collect after two years.

2) The benefit is often given as a percent of salary rather than total compensation. So, people who receive large bonuses don't get that extra benefit.

3) It's important to know whether, if on claim, the benefit goes up every year with inflation. This is important for a long-term disability.

4) You must remember who pays for the insurance. If your employer pays the premium and you go on claim, the benefit is taxable like a salary to you. If you are paying the premium the benefit would be income tax-free.

5) Figure out how long the waiting period is before you actually receive an income replacement check. Better have an emergency fund while you wait.

6) Determine whether the policy pays a benefit if you are partially disabled. Maybe you can't stand or drive all day and reduced hours cut your pay by 40 percent. In that case, can you get 40 percent of the benefit paid to you? Usually not provided with group policies.

7) Lastly the policy benefit is a percentage of salary, often around 60 percent. Be aware of this, and especially if the employer is paying the premium (taxable benefit) then you may want to supplement this on your own.

Even with a nice employer-provided group policy, though, you may still want to supplement it by purchasing your own individual portable policy. You'll be able to customize waiting period, length of benefit, and inflation protection, though the amount of income insurance you can purchase is limited (the insurance companies want to make sure you still have enough incentive to get back to work). Many individual policies pay partial benefits if you lose more than 20 percent of your income but aren't fully disabled and still working. From there, you can choose the amount of your benefit, up to the maximum the insurance company will allow based on your total income, including bonuses.

The cost of an individual disability income policy varies, and you have to be medically underwritten, but it's usually roughly 2 percent of the insured's income. So, let's do a comparison. Given the exact same job description, which salary package would you now choose?

Salary Package 1	Salary Package 2
Salary $100,000	Salary $98,000
Income if disabled: $0	Income if disabled: $70,000 until age 67

With this example now in mind, you have to ask yourself: Is my peace of mind worth that 2 percent of my income (the premium cost)?

Life Insurance

If your employer offers life insurance as a benefit, then grab it; you just may want to supplement it with a life insurance policy of your own.

There are two types of life insurance: term and permanent.

Term insurance is temporary insurance; it pays out over a certain period, or *term*, of time. That is, when you stop paying into it, then it dies right there, claimed or not. It is pure insurance in that you pay the premium and your beneficiary collects the income tax-free death benefit if you happen to have a claim (die) while you own the policy. You can get a policy with the premiums locked in for a period of years to match your needs, such as when your mortgage is paid off, your kids are out of college, or your retirement age. Think 10, 15, or even 30 years of level premiums. The longer the guaranteed period, the higher the premium.

For young healthy people, it is very inexpensive insurance, but that is because you are *very* unlikely to have a claim. Since you have to be healthy in order to get a policy, you are likely to have a very long life expectancy and outlive the term policy. If you don't have as long of a life expectancy due to health condition(s) or your age, insurers jack up the price or don't offer you insurance at all.

Furthermore, the longer a term policy is around, the higher the premiums are going to rise after the level premium period ends, until by the time you're old enough to actually need it, you can't afford the premiums and will just drop the policy.

This is why only about 2 percent of all term policies ever get claimed. Term insurance is ideal for those with tight budgets.

Permanent life insurance differs in that it sticks with you until you have a claim (die), so it's not technically insurance at all. Remember "insurance" is a transfer of risk for something unlikely to happen, and we are guaranteed to have a death claim, so it's really a way to build a long-term asset at claim time. Term insurance may be cheaper in the short-term, but perm will be there and *always* pays out to your family when the time comes. It's also better for those who want to leave their heirs some sort of financial legacy.

There are several types of perm life insurance; they differ in their rates of return, guarantees, internal expenses, and mortality charges. It can get a little confusing, but the basics are that a good perm policy can be custom-designed to fulfill your needs and be in place when you die. My current favorite is called a Guaranteed Universal Life policy; it works like a term policy but is guaranteed for your lifetime (up to 120 years as an option) at a fixed annual premium of your choice.

Additionally, here are a few benefits of permanent life insurance:

- Death benefit is inherited free from federal income tax.
- Improved life policy design allows the insured to purchase a "Guaranteed" death benefit (not subject to stock market risk) that is much cheaper than traditional "whole life" insurance because no cash value accumulates for the insurance company.

- Your average life insurance policy usually earns more interest than you can get from a certificate of deposit ("CD") investment.

- As you can see, this is a terrific way to transfer wealth to your loved ones. But when planning your insurance coverage, you have to make sure to get answers to three key questions:

- Will the income generated from my life insurance cover my family's bills?

- Will the lack of my income force my spouse to have to work more hours?

- Will it cover funeral and other expenses?

Break out the calculator, and start punching in some numbers to make sure that you have enough insurance for your family's needs.

No matter what the type of life insurance, it gets more expensive the older you get, so the sooner you start the better. Now, I have had clients in their 70s purchase life insurance with a chronic care rider for use as a wealth transfer asset, knowing that even though their payments would be higher, they would have fewer years to pay-in for, but that's not advisable for everyone. Better to get it while it's relatively cheap, especially if you have a family depending on your uninterrupted flow of paychecks.

But what if something unexpected happens before you die? What if you have an accident, sudden injury, or develop some sort of debilitating illness (dementia)? What if Al falls off the roof putting up a TV antenna for Peg? You need the money *now.* Well, now you can take an advance on your death benefit (if your policy has a chronic care rider) while you're alive to pay for chronic or long-term care expenses. To do this while you are relatively healthy, you need to make sure to buy your perm life insurance with a special rider to access your life insurance death benefit as a contingency plan for unexpected chronic conditions. Use these funds to help you get through such daily living activities you may no longer be able to perform. For Al and Peg, that rider might be a page on the policy that basically says, *"If Al gets dementia, we can start accessing the death benefit of his perm life policy with the chronic care rider any way we would like."*

Bathing, toileting, eating, dressing, even moving about the house may require help and extra materials, maybe even a bath nurse to come around and assist you. Maybe you'll need a wheelchair ramp built into your home. All of this requires money. Now, you can pay it out of your soon-to-be dwindling savings, or you can think ahead and see if your insurance company can supply this sort of rider for just such a contingency. Some companies even allow for a relative to be paid to come and assist you, as long as you have been diagnosed with a chronic illness.

In fact, life insurance with an option to use the death benefit to pay for long-term chronic care expenses may be more attractive than actual long-term care insurance. With this in place, your life insurance can cover all your chronic care costs during your retirement years. Or, more to the point, you really *need* to have such costs covered as part of your long-range retirement plan.

So, what is the right type of life insurance? The right amount? The right time to buy? That last one is an easy enough answer, so I'll handle that one first. I bought my own life insurance policy back in my mid-20s before I even had prospects of a wife, and it's benefiting me now, so the answer to that one would be "as soon as you are able." If you already do have a family, then the question becomes, "Why haven't you done this yet?" And remember that the longer you wait, the older you get, the more expensive it gets.

The answers to the other questions—what is the right type of life insurance? the right amount? —depend on your own unique circumstances. How big is your family? Remember, your spouse may have to live on this for the rest of his or her life in place of your income. For example, a $1,000,000 death benefit sounds like a lot, but if you invest it pretty conservatively for a 5 percent annual return– 4 percent after taxes– then that comes to $40,000 per year (plus any qualified social security income and other work or investments); not exactly living the Lifestyle of the Rich and Famous.

Let me leave you with a quick little chart (term and 4 different types of perm) comparing the pros and cons of each of the main types of insurance out there; that way you can judge for yourself. If you still have any questions, you can always consult with an expert such as me.

	Term	Whole Life	Universal Life	Indexed Universal Life	Variable Universal Life
Premium	Premiums start low, increase at each renewal	Level—Fixed The premium cannot be decreased or increased by policyholder	2 Types: 1) Flexible 2) Guaranteed	Flexible "Indexed" means the investment return mirrors the benchmark where the money is invested. For example, the Standard & Poor's 500 Stock Index	Flexible
Coverage	Usually renewable until at least age 70; for some policies, up to age 95	For life	For life (can be adjusted for a shorter protection duration)	For life (can be adjusted for a shorter protection duration)	For life (can be adjusted for a shorter protection duration)
Death benefit	Guaranteed	Guaranteed May increase with dividends	May be guaranteed depending on policy Can be increased or decreased	May be guaranteed depending on policy Varies relative to cash value index returns	May be guaranteed depending on policy Can be increased or decreased; varies relative to cash value investment returns
Cash value	None	Guaranteed May increase with dividends	Guaranteed minimum Varies based on interest rates	Not guaranteed Fluctuates with underlying index performance	Not guaranteed Fluctuates with underlying investment performance
Policy loans allowed?	Not applicable account	Yes. May be able to borrow up to 100 percent of total cash surrender value less annual loan interest rate	Yes	Yes	Yes
Cash value account growth	No cash value account	Insurance company determines guaranteed cash value and declares dividends based on performance of its general investment portfolio	Insurance company determines cash value interest crediting rates based on current interest rate returns to the company	Cash value account growth depends on the investment performance of the indexed account chosen	Cash value account growth depends on the investment performance of the subaccounts chosen

————————— ✐ —————————

"A long while ago, my daughter needed a couple of medical tests done to see if she was in shape for the cheerleading squad. I just hauled her over to a concierge clinic and saved enough cash to buy her uniform, with money left over to get her a nice dress for the Freshman Dance as well."

"I was eating ramen for a week paying for my daughter's dress," Steve chuckled. "And don't get me started on how much I've been paying in medical insurance even before this lovely stay here."

"Son, I'm just gettin' started. Several years ago, I ran across this thing called a Health Savings Account. Now this one's really gonna blow your mind..."

————————— ✐ —————————

Health Savings Account (HSA)

A Health Savings Account (HSA) is like an interest-bearing checking account, complete with a checkbook and debit card, but the money it holds can only be used for qualified medical expenses. HSAs are great for retirement planning. In fact, I put my HSA contribution away before my 401k when it comes to retirement savings. To be eligible to have a HSA, your medical insurance plan has to be qualified as a High Deductible Health Plan (HDHP), with a minimum $1350 deductible for individuals and $2700 for families. However, if you *do* qualify for a HSA, then there are several benefits that it will bring you:

- Contributions are fully federal-income-tax-deductible.
- No income eligibility limitations like IRA or Roth IRA.
- Any money growth while in your HSA is tax-deferred.
- Some banks allow you to invest your HSA money in a brokerage account and keep the tax benefits while in a HSA. Imagine the awesome long-term growth possibilities for this money without it ever being taxed!
- Money taken out of the HSA for IRS-approved medical expenses is tax-free. These include dentist, doctor, and hospital charges, plus prescriptions, as well as insurance premiums like Medicare and long-term-care insurance premiums.

The IRS website has a detailed list of approved medical-related expenses that qualify for tax deductible uses. I have given some parts of that list in the chart below, but for a full and current listing, you may consult the IRS website.

Common IRS-Qualified Medical Expenses

- Acupuncture
- Ambulance
- Birth control treatment
- Blood sugar test kits for diabetics
- Breast pumps and lactation supplies
- Chiropractor
- Contact lenses and solutions
- Dental treatments

- Doctors' office visits and co-pays
- Drug addiction treatment
- Drug prescriptions
- Eyeglasses (prescription and reading)
- Fertility enhancement (including in-vitro fertilization)
- Hearing aids and the batteries for the devices
- Infertility treatment
- Inpatient alcoholism treatment
- Insulin
- Laboratory fees
- Medical alert bracelet
- Medical records charges
- Orthodontics
- Orthotic Inserts (custom or off the shelf)
- Physical therapy
- Special education services for learning disabilities (recommended by a doctor)
- Speech therapy
- Stop-smoking programs (including nicotine gum or patches, if prescribed)
- Surgery, excluding cosmetic surgery
- Vaccines
- Vision exam
- Walker, cane, wheelchair

Individuals can contribute up to $3,450 annually, while $6,900 is the maximum for couples. Contributors over 55 can invest an additional $1,000. The extra bonus, finally, is that anything you put into the HSA can be left to grow over time; it stays in the account. No more "use it or lose it." Then, as long as any withdrawals are for medical expenses, everything's okay, though if you withdraw for any non-qualified reason then you are taxed and also incur a 20 percent penalty (if you're over 65, then the penalty is waived). For myself, I try to keep from spending anything in my HSA so it can keep growing tax-free. For a calculator to illustrate how much your account may grow, go to http://www.hsabank.com/hsabank/learning-center/hsa-savings-calculator.

The Elephant in the Room

How will you be able to afford living with a high deductible health insurance plan?

In exchange for the burden of having a higher deductible for your regular health insurance, the monthly premium should be much lower. Use your premium savings to fund your HSA. For a calculator to determine how much monthly premium you might save by going to a high deductible health plan, go to http://www.hsabank.com/hsabank/learning-center/compare-your-health-plans.

You'll still have those funds available for medical expenses, but meanwhile you'll be earning interest on them in your HSA account. You can set up an automatic monthly transfer of funds from your checking account into your HSA account to make sure that everything is done the way you want.

Back to Al and Peg. Al set things up so that $200 a month is automatically transferred from his checking direct into his HSA before any other bills are paid. That's $200 a month less that Peg can needle out of him because they both know it's going to something important and completely out of their hands at that point. If they leave that money alone, then after 20 years of earning 5 percent, they will have a balance of just over $66,000!

My favorite for HSAs is "HSA Bank." Besides all the usual perks expected of other medical savings accounts, these accounts also allow HSA Bank customers to open an account with TD Ameritrade so that customers can buy and sell your investments directly from within their HSAs.

"You mean I can get paid interest while saving up money for medical insurance?" Steve was incredulous, his reaction earning an even broader smile from the old man than before.

"How do you think I'm payin' for my little stay in the Hotel Healthcare here? I got myself an HSA ages ago. Now listen up, 'cause my family'll be here in a couple of hours an' I want to spend some time with them."

"Oh, of course."

At this point Steve was very much caught up with everything the old man was telling him. He fluffed his pillow and turned his full attention to Harold's next words.

Highlights

- A large emergency fund allows you the financial permission to have worry free high deductible insurance and save on premiums every year.

- Double check your vehicle and house insurance from time to time to make sure that you aren't covering more than you need to.

- For medical insurance, if a future event is unpredictable, unlikely to happen, and really expensive, then it's probably worth getting coverage for.

- For any type of insurance, raising your deductible for what would amount to small out-of-pocket expenses will save you a ton on your premiums.

- Long-term care funding solution:

  - Long-term care policies are use it (sick claim) or lose it (wasted premiums).

  - Life insurance with chronic care rider is use it or pass it (death benefit to heirs) and is a very attractive solution.

  - Chronic care rider is an extra cost and the terms vary for each insurer (be sure to understand).

  - Long-term care policy costs have been skyrocketing due to longer life expectancies.

- A Health Savings Account (HSA) is the best way to go to save up money for your retirement-age health needs.

~ Chapter Four ~

Investing

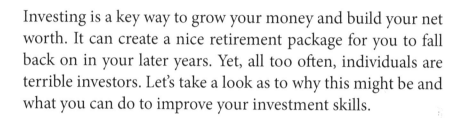

Investing is a key way to grow your money and build your net worth. It can create a nice retirement package for you to fall back on in your later years. Yet, all too often, individuals are terrible investors. Let's take a look as to why this might be and what you can do to improve your investment skills.

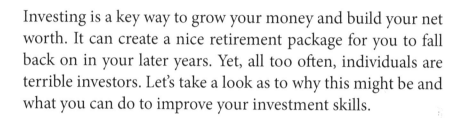

"I tried the market once," Steve confessed. "Timed it wrong and about lost my shirt. My stock started to go down, so I sold out; but then practically the very next day the price shot right back up again. Investments just aren't for me."

"Ah, then you got greedy."

"Greedy? No," Steve objected. "I just wanted to make a little extra money."

How could this old man call him greedy? Steve was just trying to get a little extra financial elbow room, same as everyone else. It's not like he was one of those big greedy corporate types.

And yet, deep inside, he had a feeling that in a way Harold might be right once again.

"Whether you realize it or not, son, you were greedy. Greed and fear, those are the two worst things for the amateur investor. It's a bit like tryin' to cross the road when you think the light might change; you could spend all day there jus' guessin' instead of doin'. Or you could make a run for it and get hit by a car."

"Then, what should I do? To use your own analogy, when should I cross the road? Just before the light turns?"

"That would be your problem, Steve. You spend too much time lookin' at the light instead of what's comin' at you in the traffic. You ever been huntin', Steve?"

"A couple of times with my father when I was a kid."

"You had to be patient, didn't you?"

"Once we had to sit for an hour just waiting for the deer to get close enough," Steve admitted.

"Well, you need to be that patient with your investments. You can't run scared, and you can't get greedy. Investments are what got me and my wife a nice little retirement package, but you have to be in it for the long haul."

"I guess that was my problem; I only gave it about two months before bailing."

"Son," Harold chuckled. "If you would have hunted the way you invest, you'd still be goin' after that deer."

Greed and Fear in Investing

Bad investing comes about from the perception that your options are more limited than you think. People try to time the market instead of spending enough time *in* the market. They try to get ahead of things, anticipate what might be coming, but like bad gamblers they fold too quickly before seeing things all the way through. They don't have the patience to be a "buy and hold" investor and end up shortchanging themselves.

The following chart demonstrates the emotional rollercoaster that individual investors go through as the value of their holding fluctuate.

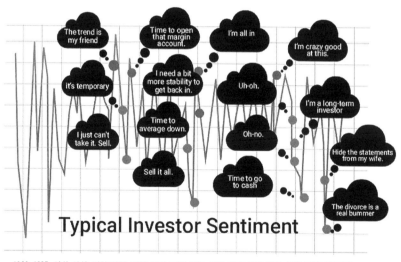

75

Next we have a cool chart that illustrates how missing the best days due to poor market timing (greed and fear play a part) costs the investor a bundle in return.

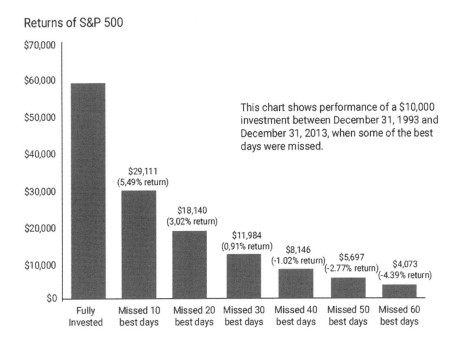

Returns of S&P 500

This chart shows performance of a $10,000 investment between December 31, 1993 and December 31, 2013, when some of the best days were missed.

So, what goes wrong? Why do otherwise smart people do so poorly when it comes to investing? We know that "buy low and sell high" is a tried and true axiom, and yet we ignore it at our peril. This is the result of two emotions that get in the way of the logic of most do-it-yourself investors.

Greed and fear.

But you aren't greedy, you say? Well, maybe not obviously so. You own a stock and then it starts skyrocketing. Naturally you wish you had some more, and so you buy more of that stock. The problem is that now you're buying it at a higher price than what you paid for your initial investment. This is a form of greed, and it will nip you in the rear every time, because each time you buy the stock at a higher price, you are chasing closer to the end of the run up in price. Eventually the market will peak, and that stock's price will either hold steady or start coming back down. At this point, anything you bought when near the peak will net very little, if any, profit. All you'll end up doing is selling it almost as quickly as you bought it. A stock on the rise will attract a lot of money once it gets noticed, but a good portion of that new money comes from these Johnny-come-lately investors buying high, who will be lucky to make any money and will, more than likely, get in just in time for the holding to drop in value before moving on to the next bandwagon.

But as bad as greed is, fear can be even worse. Once prices start falling panic sets in. You end up quickly selling out for fear that prices could just keep on plummeting. A selling frenzy soon ensues, and after you've sold out, the prices keep going down. Normally this would be a perfect time to buy some more of this stock, when it's really low, but after having just sold out, you're rather reluctant to do so. You fear the price might just keep going down and your money would be wasted.

Then of course there is the obvious possibility: What if that fall in price was just a temporary dip? What if it corrects back up? Then you've panic-sold for nothing. Either way, you're stuck on the sidelines. As you saw on the previous chart, missing a handful of really good investment days can make a huge difference in your investment return.

Between greed and fear, you are now doing the exact opposite of the old "buy low, sell high" axiom. Greed causes you to "buy high," while fear causes you to "sell low."

Let's go back to Al. He's not the brightest person when it comes to investing. In fact, he's been known to jump on every bandwagon in town.

Al (Day 1): Frank just told me about this Amalgamated Fuzz stock. It's gone up 10 points, and he's made 10,000 bucks. I've *got* to have it!"

Al (Day 5): I thought he said this stock was so great. Since I bought it, it's only gone up another 2 points. I don't get it; Frank told me he only paid two grand for it when he bought his, and he's making a killing. Now I buy in, pay 20,000 for it, and have only made a measly $200 for my troubles.

Al (Day 7): Amalgamated Fuzz is dropping! I've got to sell. I'll lose money, but it's better than losing it all.

Al (Day 8): Well, I lost 2,000 compared to what I bought it for, but at least I still have something.

Frank (Day 12): Hey Al, you know that Amalgamated Fuzz stock that dropped 8 points? Well it just went back up again. I finally sold mine and made $20,000 over what I put in.

Al (Same Day): Frank, never darken my doorstep again.

To overcome this cycle of greed and fear, you need a real investment strategy that is aligned with your investment goals and not your emotions. You need to learn to ignore the day-to-day motions of the market and keep an eye fixed on the longer time horizon. Investing without a plan is like sailing without a compass; you are doomed to sink on the rocky financial shoals.

Need proof? Investor returns are actually far lower than the mutual funds they invested in due to when they were bought and sold. Below is a chart that reflects the results of purchases and redemptions from stock mutual funds.

Fund investors' returns fall short of the market

TIME PERIOD	INVERSTORS EQUITY FUND RETURNS	STANDARD & POOR'S 500 INDEX	GAP BETWEEN S&P AND INVESTORS
30 Years	3.69%	11.11%	7.42%
20 Years	5.02%	9.22%	4.20%
10 Years	5.88%	7.40%	1.52%
5 Years	15.21%	17.94%	2.73%
12 Months	25.54%	32.41%	6.87%

Note: Through December 31, 2013

Every dollar used to purchase a mutual fund is tracked, which is why we know that the majority of money tends to come in when prices are high and go out, in the form of re-demptions, when the price is lower. As you can see, the individual investor does pretty poorly when compared to if he'd simply stuck it out for the long-term.

The average mutual fund equity investor holds onto a fund for an average of just 3.3 years. This is far too short a time frame for stock funds. The typical scenario for the average person is he buys something towards the top end of the market thinking it looks pretty good, but then when the new returns start petering out and don't match up to what he saw before, he gets disappointed and sells out too quickly. There's that fear again.

For the 20 years ending in 2013 the S&P 500 index averaged a growth of 9.22 percent per year. Now compare that with the average equity fund investor—an average of just 5.02 percent growth. That's a pretty big difference.

So how long *should* you hold onto something? That depends on if you're an *investor* or a *speculator.* In my book, holding onto a stock for anything fewer than five years makes you a speculator and not an investor. If you want to be an investor, then you need to prepare yourself for the long haul.

If you own your own home, and its value dips by a small percentage over the course of a couple of days, would you panic-sell it? Of course not, because we know those are just short-term meaningless fluctuations. The same goes for your investment purchases. You need to construct your investment portfolio to eliminate the fear of headlines and market drops that might scare you out of the market. Align your portfolio with your long-term goals and not momentary fluctuations.

"*I guess I* should *have held on longer,*" *Steve sheepishly admitted. "Did you ever have any close calls with stocks or mutual funds?*"

"*Oh, plenty, but I learned patience a long time ago. Had this one stock mutual fund that bottomed out back when the economy did; lost about half its value.*"

"*Oh my God,*" *Steve gasped. "You must have been wiped out!*"

"*Not really, son. It was a blue-chip stock mutual fund, and I knew they's the* first *things to come bouncin' back up. Sure enough, nine months later it was all back in the black.*"

"*You must have nerves of steel. I would have been a wreck. Did you have to constantly monitor its progress, or just sit on it and hope?*"

"*Well,*" *Harold said after a slight pause, "much like for huntin', there's two ways to invest. You can either actively track that deer down, or you can wait around for it to come over your way on its own. Same with investing; you can be active about it, or do what they call passive investing.*"

"*You do have a colorful way of comparing things, Harold.*"

"*Helps keep it in the front of the brain, son. Now listen up...*"

Active vs. Passive Investing

There are two different types of investing: active and passive.

Active management tries to beat the market, for a given niche, as measured by a particular market index, such as S&P 500 Index or the Russell 1000® Index. The investment is guided by a Human Manager, who makes his decisions based on prevailing market trends, the economy, political and other current events, and company-specific factors (such as earnings growth). An actively managed fund is often simply called a "managed fund."

Passive management, more commonly called Indexing, is a computer model based investment management approach based on purchasing exactly the same stocks and bonds, in the same proportions, as an index. It's considered passive because portfolio managers don't make decisions about which components to buy and sell, but simply copy the index. A fund managed by the index is called an "index fund."

So, which is better? Active managers believe they can beat the Index, and sometimes they do, while passive managers believe it's too expensive and not worth the cost. Each style has its advantages and disadvantages.

Actively Managed Funds

Advantages	Disadvantages
Expert analysis: Seasoned money managers may make informed decisions based on their experience, judgment, and prevailing market trends.	Higher fees and operating expenses Usually less tax efficient
Possibility of higher-than-index returns: Managers aim to beat the performance of the index.	Mistakes may happen: There is always the risk that managers may make unwise choices on behalf of investors, which could reduce returns.
Defensive measures: Managers can make changes if they believe the market may take a downturn.	Style issues may interfere with performance: At any given time, a manager's style may be in or out of favor with the market, which could reduce returns.

Passively Managed Funds

Advantages	Disadvantages
Low operating expenses Returns match those of their benchmarked index. Tax efficient	Performance dictated by index: Investors must be satisfied with market returns because that is the best any index fund can do.
No action required: There is no decision making required by the manager.	Lack of control: A few large companies often make up a large position of index and should they have a fallout, the index drops with them and there is the ability to move out of those positions.

Which is better? Wall Street is still debating that question. From time to time one or the other will work better and have its favorable points. Here is a brief bit of summarized history showing how each option performed during various market ups and downs.

	Returns of Active Managers[2]	S&P 500[1] Returns
Market Cycle (04/00 - 12/14)	7.24%	4.15%
Tech Bubble Decline (04/00 - 09/02)	-11.02%	-20.56%
Failed Recovery (10/02 - 10/07)	17.26%	15.54%
Credit Crisis (11/07 - 02/09)	-40.43%	-41.39%
Current Bull Market (03/09 - 12/14)	20.42%	21.87%

As an individual investor, you need to ignore the trends, because in the end both types of management are selecting investments from the same pool of equities. Investor returns are influenced far more by portfolio allocation and buying and selling decisions than they are by the type of management you select. Which is better for you depends on what you want, how patient you are, and if you can live with the cons vs. the pros.

I think a key consideration, though, is this: How concerned are you with risk control? If risk control is a significant consideration, then you should go with an actively managed fund. That gives you the best way of riding out a volatile market if you have a good manager with a proven track record.

Especially as you get older, though, you are more concerned with protecting your assets from a major decline, since you have less time to make up for that than before. People in this situation want a well-diversified portfolio, appropriate managers or indexes, a systematically rebalanced portfolio, and a qualified investment advisor monitoring the risk-adjusted performance of each and every investment. This takes time, talent, and a special temperament.

In the end, though, passive investing may be a bit of a misnomer, as there is no such thing as a truly passive investing strategy.

"For myself, I went for active investing," Harold grinned. "I liked having managers with a really good track record at the helm of my investments. But I realize that's not for everyone."

"I'm still not sure if investing is for me," Steve said with a shake of his head.

"Fair enough question," Harold shrugged. "You're afraid you might lose everything."

"Well... I might."

Harold paused momentarily in thought before addressing Steve with a question.

"Back when you was huntin', did you ever unload your full load of ammo all at once at that deer?"

"Of course not. We had to save some for later in case we missed or something else came up."

"Then why are you assuming that investing means you have to shoot everything you have into it all at once? However much you can afford to flush down a toilet right now, that's your buffer. Me and the wife took about a full week figurin' what our buffer was before I invested one thin dime. After that you only need to start gettin' worried when something eats into your buffer too much; until then, just sit back and keep sippin' your sweet tea. Enjoy life."

"I guess that's something I've been missing out on a lot of... Life."

"Life is what it's all about, son. Not worryin' about which investment's about to go belly-up first."

On that issue Steve had to agree. He imagined himself sitting on a porch with his wife, a glass of iced tea for each, just watching the sun go down on a lazy July afternoon.

The Most Important Question to Ask Yourself

The most important question to ask yourself is this: How much money can I afford to lose on paper without panic-selling?

This is a question you need to answer *before* the next big drop in the market. And there *will* be one, just as there will be a recovery. It may not be as bad as the 50 percent drop in 2008, but are you able to stomach even a 10 percent drop? 5 percent?

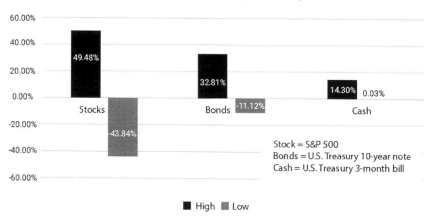

Volatility is the price paid for higher long-term returns

Stock = S&P 500
Bonds = U.S. Treasury 10-year note
Cash = U.S. Treasury 3-month bill

Source: the Federal Reserve database in St. Louis (FRED)

Software exists that can show you what would happen to your portfolio during a given market drop in terms of dollars and percentages of your current portfolio holdings. I have such software, and I'm sure that other managers have it, too. The point is, you can use this as a way of seeing how much of a market drop you're able to stomach.

As an example, I ran my software of a sample portfolio that is invested 79 percent in stocks to illustrate how it would have performed under the conditions of 2008. A loss of 37 percent!

Current Allocation

This page shows how an Investment Portfolio might be currently allocated among the different Asset Classes.

Current Portfolio

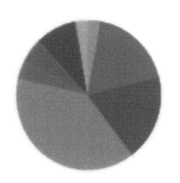

Total Stock
79%

Projected Returns

Total Return
7.88%

Bear Market Returns

Great Recession
November 2007 thru February 2009
-37%

Bond Bear Market
July 1979 thru February 1980
10%

More

Investment Portfolio

Asset Class	Rate of Return	Current	
		Value	% of Total
Short Term Bonds	1.50%	$27,500	3%
Intermediate Term Bonds	3.50%	$180,000	18%
Large Cap Value Stocks	9.00%	$180,000	18%
Large Cap Growth Stocks	9.00%	$380,000	39%
Small Cap Stocks	9.50%	$38,750	4%
International Developed Stocks	9.00%	$52,500	5%
International Emerging Stocks	10.00%	$88,750	9%
Mid. Cap. Stock Blend	9.00%	$27,500	3%
Total :		$975,000	100%

If this was similar to your portfolio allocation back in 2007-08, I hope you hung on and didn't panic sell, as the rebound during the next decade and counting has been stupendous!

The point of going through such an analysis is peace of mind. If you decided ahead of time that you could live with a 37 percent drop in value, then you can sleep soundly any time you hear of a 10 percent market drop in the news. If, however, your portfolio is not deemed secure enough against what you would view as reasonable fluctuations, then you need to talk with your investment advisor about what changes you need to make to strengthen your portfolio.

Al and Peg have some extra money they'd like to invest, but Peg is smart enough to start asking the right questions, like how much of a dip they can afford their investments to make when it comes down to it. After consulting their portfolio manager and their bank account, they realize they can only afford a 5 percent drop before things get serious. Since the stock market is known to fluctuate by much more than that, this has Peg booting Al out of the room so she can talk to the advisor about making some allocation changes to their portfolio so they have a more realistic margin like 12 to 15 percent.

"Stocks and bonds have always confused me," Steve said at one point. *"Is there really a difference between the two?"*

"Well, it's been my experience that bonds are a little like that tortoise; you can depend on it to get you there, just don't expect

it to be real soon. Stocks, on the other hand, are more like the hare; they got their risks, sure, but you'll end up crossin' the finish line a lot sooner."

"Harold, you do seem to have a way with words."

"That's what my wife said the night I asked her to be my wife," he replied with a wink. "That was right before I showed her what else I have a way with."

Stocks vs. Bonds

Stocks are ownership and bonds are loanership... When you own a stock or a stock mutual fund, you own a tiny part of the company—or companies—that you invested in. A bond is simply a loan. You can loan money to the federal government (U.S. Treasury Bond), a state municipality, a corporation, or even an international or emerging market government. In all cases, you loan the entity money in exchange for a contractual fixed interest rate, for a stated period of years, and are expected to receive a return of your principal at the end of the period.

Personally, I prefer stocks over bonds, and I'll tell you why.

Since 1926, with all the ups and downs in the market, large stocks have returned an average of roughly 9.5 percent per year; long-term government bonds have returned about 5 percent, according to the Federal Reserve. Along the way, the stock market has had wild fluctuations in prices compared to bonds. Bonds offer limited upside returns. Investors collect the dividends from the bond and may make more money if interest rates go down after they have purchased their bond(s). When interest rates stay flat then your bond price isn't going anywhere either. With bonds nowadays earning 3 to 4 percent or less, it just doesn't seem that attractive compared to a conservative estimate of the 6 to 9 percent upside for long-term stock returns. Keep in mind that for your retirement investments, your time frame is not your retirement age, but your life expectancy age, hopefully very long-term.

Let's take a look at two arguments in favor of being a bond investor: diversification and safety.

- **Diversification**: If you own assets that don't go down, or perhaps go up in value when interest rates drop, then this insulates you from some of the pain that goes with being an "owner" of companies as with stocks. The pain from seeing your account value significantly drop in value could bring about that fear response again and cause you to "sell low," which, as we have discussed, is not something you're likely to psychologically recover from no matter how good the market does afterwards.

- **Safety**: Bonds are safe relative to the lendee's ability to pay the interest owed and return your principle investment when the loan comes due. While you're holding bonds or bond mutual funds, the biggest factor regarding their perceived safety is what happens to interest rates after you purchase the bonds or bond mutual fund. If interest rates move down, as they have generally done for the past 30 years, bond prices go up, but the opposite happens when interest rates go back up.

I do not anticipate interest rates skyrocketing any time soon, as the Federal Reserve seems to be manipulating the money supply to keep interest rates low for the foreseeable future. Including bonds and other non-stock investments in your portfolio, though, should help to minimize the downside volatility from your stock investments, which protects you from that panic response.

The *duration*, stated in years, of a bond is defined as the change in the value of a fixed income security bond that will result from a 1 percent change in interest rates. For example: a five-year duration means the bond price will decrease in value by 5 percent if interest rates rise 1 percent, and increase in value by 5 percent if interest rates fall 1 percent.

Example: If your bond was worth $10,000 and interest rates went from 2.8 up to 3 percent (a change of .2 percent) then $10,000 x .02 = a $200 change. Your bond value would have dropped to $9,800. This is an approximation.

This bond duration is a very important measure for investors to consider, as bonds with higher durations carry more risk and have higher price volatility than bonds with lower durations. There are some other details, but that's the gist of it.

Something to think about if you own bonds or bond mutual funds: If the bonds you own pay a very low interest rate (and most do these days) consider cashing them in and paying down your mortgage with the proceeds. Also, rather than adding to your bond portfolio, use the money you would have added to bonds and also use it to pay down your mortgage. Having a mortgage is less attractive for many people since the new tax law was passed minimizing the mortgage interest deductibility on your tax return.

"You can't be afraid of investing, boy. Like I told each of my own children, it's not money you're investing in, it's your future. Money is just the tool that you need to get to that future. You understand what I'm sayin'?"

"I think so," Steve replied. "I just have to be careful how I go about it."

"Like ridin' a bike. There's a right way and a wrong way. Both ways'll get you to where you wanna go, but only one of them will leave you a lot less battered up."

Steve reached for his own glass of water on his nightstand, and as he was sipping and thinking over the old man's words, for a moment he imagined the water was sweet tea instead.

Highlights

- Greed and fear create terrible investing decisions.
- There are two types of investing: active and passive.
  - Actively managed funds have managers leading decision-making.
  - Passively managed funds have low operating expenses and match benchmark returns.
- It is important to determine how much money you can afford to lose, and the volatility risk, before entering into an investment.
- Stocks vs. Bonds:
  - Stocks are ownership.
  - Bonds are loans you make.
  - Bonds often provide financial insulation against stock market drops.
  - The duration of a bond measures how the bond price will fluctuate with a 1 percent change in interest rates.
  - Risks of bonds may be reduced by keeping maturity dates short-term.
  - Paying off your mortgage may be a better alternative to bond investments.

Chapter Five

Grow Net Worth with Zero Investment Taxes

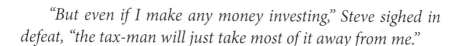

"But even if I make any money investing," Steve sighed in defeat, *"the tax-man will just take most of it away from me."*

He heard no answer at first, so Steve slowly turned his head around for a look. Harold was calmly lying back, smiling.

"Okay, old man, what do you know? Some special loophole for the rich?"

"Didn't I tell you that I ain't rich? No, there's no loopholes or special privileges. Just knowin' what's what about the way investment and taxes go. Like this one time when I was a kid, me and some other boys was trackin' down a raccoon. He was a wily little rascal that just kept escaping everyone who tried to go after him. Of course, once we began studying his habits, where he liked to hold up, and when he liked to come out, well, capturing him was just a matter of getting ahead of him. Same with taxes; you just have to know its habits to get ahead of it."

"Quick aside, but... What were you hunting a raccoon for in the first place?"

"Oh, that...I just bet that know-it-all John Hammer that I could. Craftiest raccoon in the county, but I caught him. Gave him as a present to Mary Elizabeth to keep as a pet."

"A raccoon as a pet? What did she think of that?"

"Well," Harold chuckled, "she married me, didn't she?"

We all work hard for our money, but it seems as though the government works equally hard to find ways to take it from us in the form of taxes. Not that I have anything against the government doing what it needs to do, but many times they aren't exactly the best at managing other people's money, least of all mine. With the uncertainty of what the Feds might try next to manage the ever-accelerating über-debt, it remains our task to minimize what we pay them when tax time rolls around.

In this case, I'm talking investment taxes.

With the way the government spends money, ever-expanding entitlement programs, and the debt mushrooming out of control, you could confiscate *all* the wealth from the top 1 percent of the richest people in the nation and not make a dent in that debt. You can bet that taxes are going up eventually, so stay on top of that topic.

Rule #1: It is not what you make that matters, but how much you keep.

You could have the best-looking investment on the planet, but how good is it really if the minute you cash out the government ends up with a big chunk of it? You need to find that sweet spot of good investment returns while minimizing the resulting income taxes. That's what this chapter is about.

The first thing to be aware of is the difference between *taxable, tax-deferred,* and *tax-free,* because not all taxes are created equal. Taxable, of course, means that you get hit with an income tax every year on what you make, while tax-free is just what it says but *only* if the funds in the given type of investment are used as indicated for that investment. So, a 529 tax-free college savings plan remains tax-free if spent on qualified school needs but not for buying yourself a new car, or the funds in a Health Savings Account stay clear of the tax man as long as the money is spent on qualified medical needs. Finally, tax-deferred means that the tax is put off until later. So, if you have a tax-deferred investment plan, that means instead of being taxed at the end of every year for any gains in that account that year, you are only taxed on the gains when you finally cash out.

These are important distinctions to remember, since they could spell the difference between being taxed a little or a whole lot more. For instance, suppose you're invested in a mutual fund that's not tax-deferred; you pay tax every year that mutual fund distributes a capital gain or dividend. The accumulated tax for this could add up to more than if you were just able to defer it and only pay at the end of that 10-year period on what the final net gain turned out to be.

So, how can you minimize income taxes on your investments? Well, the first thing is to know what you are investing the money *for*. There is a difference between general savings, retirement, college, and health needs; for each there is a specific type of investment plan that you can best use to put away money for that need and minimize or eliminate any taxes you would normally incur for that amount. But you have to plan ahead and decide how you're going to partition your investments based on your needs. After that, it's just a matter of matching the need with the best tax-advantaged wrapper for your investment.

In all cases, you need to look ahead, plan out your investment carefully, and calculate just what sort of percentage you'll actually be left with at the end. The type of investment plan you're in will dictate how you'll be taxed and when. As it turns out, some of the more popular investments end up being some of the worst when it comes to taxes.

The Problem with Mutual Funds

In the case of mutual funds outside of your qualified retirement plan, they might look good but may be hiding nasty surprises you'll learn of only when you get your 1099 at the end of the year. It is not uncommon to see your account fail to grow much in value for a given year, and yet you're taxed on a huge amount that bears no resemblance to your reality. How does this happen?

Well, you may have just started investing in that stock mutual fund only two years ago, but the fund itself has been going on for a lot longer than that. A given fund could have investments in as many as 100 different companies, and throughout the year its manager will buy or sell stock and have to report the resulting gains or losses, which are then passed onto the fund's investors. So, the fund itself could have bought some Apple stock way back when it was just $20 a share, then 10 years later sold it for a whopping $100 per share; the tax paid by the investors is then based on that huge gain. But you could have just bought into this fund two years ago when Apple was $98 a share. You only see a profit of $2 a share but are paying taxes as if you'd seen the full $80 a share profit.

That's the sort of trouble you can get into if you don't understand how investments are taxed.

Index Mutual Funds

These are one tax efficient alternative form of a mutual fund. Given that it is a passive investment, there are fewer security sales (generating taxable capital gains) and this makes it more tax efficient than most managed mutual funds.

Exchange Traded Fund (ETF)

The best solution there is to the problem with mutual funds is an ETF. There are two main differences between an ETF and a regular mutual fund. First, an ETF fund is indexed, and there is very little in the way of sales, so fewer capital gains accumulate. More significant, however, is how the sale of ETFs is handled.

For a regular mutual fund, when the investor wants to cash out, the manager sells securities to raise the necessary cash, and, of course, any profit gets taxed, which the investor then has to pay. But in an ETF, what you are really selling is your interest in the ETF to another potential investor; no actual stocks are sold, so there's nothing from there to get taxed on. The fund's manager handles the transfer of power—finding a new investor to buy your share in the ETF—then gives you that money on which your tax is then based.

It's a bit like the difference between selling a house versus selling just the *key* to the house and letting the house stay in the name of someone like "My Home, Inc." The house stays put; it's just the key that changes hands. Not an exact analogy, I'll admit, but I hope it paints the correct picture.

ETFs end up being far more efficient when it comes to taxes, plus they usually have lower internal expenses since they have no management teams involved.

Tax Managed Portfolio

This is another solution to the problem with mutual funds and the capital gains they pass onto their shareholders. In a tax managed portfolio, there is a coordination and communication that normal mutual funds lack, which allows managers to take portfolio losses to offset those gains, leaving investors with little to no capital gain tax to pay. A terrific way to get some tax-deferred growth.

What May be Wrong with a Traditional 401k?

The answer to this question, in short, is potentially a lot. While I love the paycheck deduction feature, since this gets people to save money, when you eventually withdraw money, that amount will be taxed based on what the tax rate is whenever you make that withdrawal. With the historic new tax law passed in 2017, which lowered everybody's income tax brackets, you may never be in a lower tax bracket than you are today. That tax benefit of your 401k payroll deduction is based on the tax you would have paid on that money if you had not saved it.

2018 tax brackets

Single filers		Married filers	
10%	$0-$9,525	10%	$0-$19,050
12%	$9,526-$38,70	12%	$19,051-$77,400
22%	$38,701-$82,500	22%	$77,401-$165,000
24%	$82,501-$157,500	24%	$165,001-$315,000
32%	$157,501-$200,000	32%	$315,001-$400,000
35%	$200,001-$500,000	35%	$400,001-$600,000
37%	$500,001 or more	37%	$600,001 or more
Standard deducation:	$12,000	Standard deducation:	$24,000
Personal Exemption:	Eliminated	Personal Exemption:	Eliminated

You could be taking a deduction at a low tax rate, then, if tax rates go up in the future, pay at a higher rate when you take your money out of your 401k.

You do not know what the tax rate will be years from now, so there is no way to plan ahead to account for it. It could be 35 percent, in which case the value of your million-dollar account could be worth only $650,000 after tax. This is never figured into your annual statements; the surprise comes at the end in the form of a "surrender charge" (income tax) that could suddenly lop off as much as one-third of what you thought you had. If you started your 401k at a time when federal income taxes were low, that says nothing about what will happen later. If the taxes suddenly increase about the time you hit 59-and-a-half and are ready to cash out, you could be in a lot of trouble.

A better option may be a Roth 401k. Here are some differences between a Roth 401k and a traditional 401k:

- With a Roth 401k, you do not get to deduct your contribution on your annual tax return. Sounds bad, but wait for it…

- When you take out the money after age 59-and-a-half, it is then *tax-free.*

- If you roll your 401k into a Roth IRA, which I will soon explain, you will not be subject to Required Minimum Distribution (RMD) after age 70-and-a-half.

Yes, that's right! No worrying about what the future income tax rate will be like, that's all said and done; just a lump sum of cash. You can't get that with a traditional 401k or IRA.

Similar to this is the Roth IRA. It works just the same, saving investors $5,000 per year of after-tax money, growing tax-deferred until age 59-and-a-half when it can be withdrawn tax-free. Here's a quick summary of points for the Roth IRA:

- No tax on the account growth.
- No tax if you withdraw the money after age 59-and-a-half.
- There is no RMD, and you are not forced to withdraw the funds once you hit 70-and-a-half years old.
- Anything that is unspent upon the holder's death passes to the account's beneficiaries tax-free.
- You can contribute directly if your joint income with your spouse is under a certain amount (currently $189,000); this is phased out after your joint income gets too high (currently above $199,000). These limitations creep higher over time.
- You can convert an existing IRA account that has never been taxed into a Roth IRA. You would still have to count the amount converted as ordinary income and pay tax, but after that, no more taxes on it again.
- If you withdraw prior to age 59-and-a-half, you can still do so if the money is needed for one of the following:
  - Medical expenses
  - College tuition
  - Funeral expenses
  - Funds needed to avoid eviction or foreclosure on your primary residence

Your employer's traditional 401k is nice because you never see the money, and it's better if it comes with a matching contribution, but beware of the lurking tax you have pay when you want your money. There may be better options.

103

529 College Savings Plan

I only briefly mentioned this in a previous chapter, but a 529 college savings plan is an excellent device for saving up for your kids' college plans tax-free. In this plan, you pay *zero* tax on the growth of the money invested while in this account, then when you pull it out to pay for college, there is once again *zero* tax owed. You get to put money away, watch it grow, and never pay any taxes on it ever again. Once the kids are out of high school, you can then withdraw money from the account for any qualified educational expenses, again *tax-free*.

The beneficiary can be changed among family members, and you should know that your 529 plan money is not com-mingled with your state's money (no one here in Illinois wants our broke state to be able to touch their 529 plan money!), and you can use your account balance for any college-related ex-penses in any state.

Additionally, some states allow you to get a tax deduction on what you contribute to this plan, up to a certain limit. For the state of Illinois, this is $10,000 for an individual or $20,000 for a joint tax return. I've relied heavily on this for the funding of my three children's college educations.

Health Savings Account (HSA)

I've mentioned this one before in a lot more detail, so I won't belabor it again, but I want to give a quick little remind-er about HSAs in the context of investment taxes. With contri-butions being deductible on federal income taxes, zero tax paid on the growth of the account, and zero tax on qualified medical expenses, this is a nice little tax haven for those medical emergencies you're worried about. In my case, I save around $8,000 a year in premiums by keeping my deductible high, paying just $350 a month for my family of five. I take a portion of that health insurance premium savings and put $6,900 per year into my HSA. I also take full advantage of investing my balance into a portfolio of investments aimed to grow for the long-term. Maybe one day they'll come up with bionic joints, and I'll be able to play basketball for ever.... I'll need as much in this account as possible.

Again, this is the best tax haven for you when you want an investment that will be there for future medical emergencies.

Permanent Life Insurance

I've also mentioned perm life insurance in a lot more detail than I will give here. But it's important to discuss this again in the context of taxes. Suffice it to say here that it is a good tax haven, as well as a good little nest egg for your family for when that final day comes. With a cash value policy, the growth of its cash value is tax-deferred, and if you need to get to the cash value for something, you can withdraw up to the amount of the premium tax-free, or borrow against the death benefit tax-free before taking action. (Every policy is different, so be sure to get all the details and understand any ramifications.) I did this several years ago when I needed $40,000 to pay for an addition onto our house. It's the ideal legacy asset, as death benefits passed to survivors are also tax-free.

There's no immediate tax deduction involved, but with all those tax deferrals, it doesn't really matter. This has always been a foundational component of my financial plan.

Other Low-Tax Investments

Let's wrap this chapter up with some other types of investments that are worth a quick note. Like everything else mentioned in this chapter, if you want to learn the details on how to get some of these options set up, just go to a good investment counselor for some help.

- Non-dividend paying growth stocks: These are stocks that don't pay a dividend, so nothing to tax there, but when you sell them after they've grown in value enough, the tax you pay is a preferential capital gains rate. This means lower taxes if you don't mind waiting for the stock to increase enough.

- Municipal bonds: Municipal bonds are issued by state municipalities. If your state is not a financial disaster like some, then you can loan money to the state and the interest you earn will be federally tax-free. It may be a better idea to invest in an ETF, index fund, or mutual fund that is made up of a diversified portfolio of municipal bonds that will generate federally tax-free monthly income.

- Commercial real estate: There are entire books written on this subject. Investment properties that generate positive cash flow are especially attractive because the tax laws allow for depreciation (phantom expense) to offset the net rental cash flow income. Also, the property appreciation is tax-deferred, and when you sell a property you can either pay a capital gains tax or roll the proceeds into another property to continue with the tax deference (1031 exchange). If you're interested in this, then I would advise doing some research then consulting with a specialist.

"That's quite a few options," Steve admitted. "I never would have thought of half that stuff. But how do you keep it all straight?"

"I admit to having had a few consultations with some experts on the subject," Harold shrugged. "At this point, though, after putting five kids through college as well as a few grandkids, not to mention my well-funded fading years, I've been into it long enough to just have it all memorized. Of course, I try to keep up on any changes as they come along. Don't suppose I'll have to do that anymore, though. Now it's all in the hands of my kids, bless 'em all."

So caught up in the conversation had Steve become that he had nearly forgotten about why either one of them was there in the hospital to begin with. Here they both were, so near to death, and yet all Steve could see in Harold was blissfulness; the bliss that comes with knowing that everything has been taken care of.

How Steve was beginning to envy that bliss.

Highlights

- It is not what your investment makes that matters, but how much you keep.
- Mutual funds may pass on unexpected taxes.
- ETFs avoid the capital gains pitfalls of regular mutual funds.
- A tax-managed portfolio is another alternative to regular mutual funds.
- A Roth 401k has several tax advantages over a 401k:
  - No tax if you withdraw the money after age 59-and-a-half.
  - You aren't forced to withdraw the funds once you hit age 70-and-a-half if rolled over to Roth IRA.
  - Anything unspent (and converted to a Roth IRA) passes to the account's beneficiaries tax-free.
  - When you take out the money after age 59-and-a-half, it is then *tax-free*.
- Other tax-efficient investment tax growth vehicles include:
  - 529 college savings plans for your kids' college years
  - Health Savings Account
  - Permanent life insurance
  - Non-dividend paying growth stocks
  - Municipal bonds
  - Commercial real estate

Chapter Six

Planning for Successful Retirement

———————— ⌇ ————————

Retirement is a relatively new thing that dates back to the creation of Social Security (1930s) as a means of transitioning older unproductive workers out of the hard labor jobs to make room for the younger workers. Back then the average life expectancy was about age 62, but social security benefits didn't start paying out until age 65.

It's a far different world now. The 1980s brought the creation in the tax code of the 401k to draw lots of money into the banking institutions in the form of retirement savings; so one could save up for a life of leisure after they couldn't work anymore. Needless to say, the concept of retirement has its downsides. You spend your life focusing on retiring with some means but in the end, find very little actual meaning. Early death, diminishing health, and sheer boredom are some of the results of retirement, not to mention a spike in the divorce rates.

The take-home message here is that focusing on retirement over financial independence is a really *bad* idea. If you're in a hurry to retire then it may mean that you hate your job and should get out *now*. Take the time to think about how you're spending your time, then find something you like doing and a way to get paid doing it. You'll be happier, which leads to healthier, and in no hurry to retire, which means a better chance for financial independence.

It was still dark outside, but the suggestion of dawn was not too far away when Steve asked his next question.

"So, how did you plan for your retirement?"

"Retirement?! If I would have spent half my life just focusing on my retirement, then when would I have had time to live? I've been to the Grand Canyon, Yosemite, and Mexico. My kids grew up with trips all up and down the coast, and I was honored to have many a fine experience with my wife."

"But if you didn't plan for your retirement, then how—"

"I said I didn't plan for my retirement, I didn't say that I hadn't planned for my future. There's plenty of time to retire once you're six feet under... And I'm guessin' that by this time tomorrow I might finally just retire."

"What I mean is, that after 30 or 40 years on the job, you finally want—"

"A change? I've changed careers many times in my life, son; if I got tired of doing something, I just moved on instead of waiting a few decades for some gold watch and a pat on the back. For

most people, planning for retirement seems to mean that you're planning for your death, and who wants to waste 40 years of his life doin' that? Nah, what I did was plan for contingencies for the day when I might be too mortal for my own good. Plenty of things to put on the list, but once you've gotten it all taken care of, then you can spend those 30 or 40 years enjoying yourself and your family. You just need to balance the living in today with what you need for the future. Now isn't that a sight better than planning for 'retirement?'"

Steve sighed and shook his head. He was well past embarrassment now and into feeling truly humbled.

"Harold, I thought I knew everything, but I can't even call myself an old fool now; I'm just a fool."

"Naw, you're just a young whippersnapper, is all. If I would have planned for my retirement, then I would have run out of money about 25 years ago. I'm 90-years-old, so pay attention..."

What to Plan For

So, when you're planning for "retirement," you're really planning for the day when you want to walk away from it all and relax. A day when you've built up enough savings so you don't have to work but can live off of what you have. Of course, before that day comes, you have to figure out if you'll have enough money at that time to cover your regular living expenses, which means that you need to figure out what those living expenses will be in the first place.

111

Start by making a list of your monthly expenses, then figure out what you might be paying on each of them after you retire. Remember that this may be a number of years from now, so you'll have to do some extrapolating. Here's a quick list to get you started on what you should be considering:

- Mortgage
- Property taxes
- Home owner's insurance
- Utilities
- Clothing
- Food and entertainment
- Gifts
- Car payments
- Auto insurance
- Travel
- Medicare
- Life and long-term care insurance

Now you know what you'll need to be shelling out every month, time to compare to what you expect to be earning from your assorted retirement accounts. Take the estimated income from your social security, 401k, IRAs, and any pension you might be lucky enough to be receiving. If your income is greater than those expenses up there, then you're doing well. Of course, you have to remember to calculate any *taxes* you'll have on your retirement income, and that is where a lot of people usually fall. That's why a number of retirees continue working part-time.

After you've totaled up your post-retirement income, how much of it can you then pull out to cover your monthly expenses without digging into the principal? The usual rule of thumb is 4 percent. So, if you have a $1,000,000 investment balance, then you should be able to pull out $40,000 every year from that. Simple enough to calculate, except that there are some flaws in the old 4 percent rule.

First off, like for any rule of thumb you need to customize it for your own particular situation. Some people live entirely off their pensions, others continue to work part-time and hardly touch their investments, while still others need to systematically spend some of their principal every year.

The 4 percent rule came about years ago when CDs were paying nearly 5 percent, so you could lock in your principle at a higher rate than you were drawing from. Nowadays, though, you'd be lucky to find something in the 2 percent to 3 percent range. That makes it a bit tricky to plan your financial security around a hard and fixed 4 percent rule.

And, remember what I said before about getting taxed on that retirement income? The old 4 percent rule was usually figured before taking taxes into account. Do you know what income taxes will be like when you retire? Thought not.

Know what else has changed since retirement was invented? Life expectancy. Living longer means you have many healthier years that you need to plan for, and those fixed rules of thumb may simply not be up to it. Suddenly, increased longevity just became a financial risk.

> Suddenly, increased longevity just became a financial risk

The Longevity Risk

It used to be easy; work until 65, plan on dying around 70, and work your finances around that. But now 65 is the new 55, and you're better off planning on living into your 90s. That puts more of a strain on your long-term plans for financial independence. You need to adjust your plans accordingly.

First, plan on working past 65. Even if it's just part-time, that could make a significant difference on your finances. You're still feeling young with all the energy, so why not use it? Also, for people born after 1960, you won't qualify for your full social security benefits until you reach age 67.

You can also move to a low-tax state. Not every state has the same property and state income taxes; some are actually more favorable to retirees than others. There's a very good reason why places like Florida are popular places for retirement.

Don't rely on investment returns being as high in the future as they might be right now. Start saving more money *now*; then you'll have a lot more to work with *later.*

The cost of living is also going to change over the course of your long life. As such, you need to make sure that your investment portfolio takes this into account. When you retool your investment portfolio, remember that health care is likely to be your single biggest future expense.

But don't just look at healthcare when analyzing your investment portfolio. Many people make the mistake of reallocating their retirement money to match their retirement age.

Don't do that; you will not suddenly be withdrawing all your money on the day that you retire. That money will be invested for your entire lifetime (joint lifetime if married), which means we could be talking a 20- to 40-year horizon.

Living longer is great, but it carries with it the responsibility of planning ahead for it. That's not the only mistake in retirement planning, of course. There are a few others.

"I swear, the first time I retired—"

"What do you mean 'first time?' How many times can you retire?"

Harold just grinned and continued.

"When I retired, I wanted to do all sorts of things at once. Problem is, you can't do that and still have money left over. A good friend of mine, when he retired, started splurging something awful, and before he knew it, he was broke. Back to livin' on ramen like some college kid."

Harold shook his head at the recollection, perhaps wondering how his old friend ever came out.

"But, didn't you want to… Well, do things? Go places?"

"Sure, but no use goin' hog wild about it. I spent a lot of time savin' up all that money, and I planned on taking a long time to spend it…"

Don't Make These Mistakes

There are three main things you can do wrong when planning for your financial independence. These are common mistakes that a lot of people make, which is why I'm including them here.

The first mistake is a really big one; I call it "Retirement Euphoria." You've spent all those years working and planning, and suddenly you have access to a five or six figure account and want to splurge. You can't take it with you when you die, of course, but don't spend it all in one place either. Avoid being frivolous and take a longer view of your financial situation. Make sure your basic needs are covered first, then add in your wants, and see if those desires are still something your social security and pension can cover; if not, then you know how much you need to generate from your portfolio, and from there how much you can spare on that little bit of euphoria.

The second common mistake is forgetting about the likelihood of needing assistance in your old age. No one ever thinks about needing this, so most people skip over this part, but you avoid it at your peril. Say something doesn't go as expected, Al comes down with cancer or Peg finds more parts of her body breaking down than expected—they could find themselves spending their entire savings in just a few short years. But you can avoid that. Your plans need to include the handling of long-term care whether you think you'll need it or not.

Finally, and most important, do not rely solely on bonds or CDs to generate income. Like I said before, the time of CD greatness has come and gone. Nowadays you'd be lucky to get one with a 3 percent return, and more than likely get something in the 1 to 2 percent range. That's not anything to plan a life around; you need a far more diversified portfolio.

So, with that said, let's take a look at some other options available for your retirement investment portfolio.

A Paid Off Mortgage is Key

As you go over your expected retirement-year expenses, you will no doubt find that the single biggest expense will be your mortgage (if you have one). It's bigger than your property taxes, it's bigger than your utility bills, bigger than your insurance costs... combined. No plan can bring you complete financial independence until that mortgage is history.

You could always pay it off with some of your investment money. Of course, that may greatly decrease the size of your nest egg, not to mention the taxes for pulling the money out of your IRA. A better way to plan would be to refinance your mortgage to match your final mortgage pay-off year with the year of your retirement. You'll often get a lower interest rate and a higher payment to make every month, though it *will* be paid off a lot quicker. How to handle this?

Look upon your mortgage payment as what you would have put into bonds instead. You'll be using that money to pay down something that has an interest rate higher than what many bonds could give you in return to make up for it, which means that overall you'll be saving money.

Here's an example: Al has a $300,000 mortgage at a 4 percent fixed rate. He also holds bonds worth $300,000 that pay out at a 2 percent rate. By the time all is said and done, he's *losing* 2 percent. On the other hand, if he skips the bonds and puts his money into getting the mortgage paid off as quickly as he can, then he hits retirement with no outgoing mortgage payment, which makes Peg happy.

Of course, after you retire you could always use your investment income for your mortgage payments. Say you have $500,000 in investments and take out 4 percent per year, after taxes that could come to about $1500 per month. That's just enough to cover your mortgage payment, never mind anything else. That's a lot of investment to waste on mortgage payments, so let's try again.

This is where you have to plan ahead. As in *now*.

1) Refinance your loan for a shorter payoff. You'll get lower interest with higher monthly payments but have it all done and over with by retirement.

2) Start making extra payments to your mortgage company. Got some extra money this month? Throw it on the mortgage.

3) Set up an investment account and make monthly additions so you'll eventually be able to use that money to pay off the mortgage early.

4) If there is no better way, then downsize at retirement. Do you really need a house that big anymore? Then sell it, pay off the mortgage all in one go, and use the extra profit to get yourself a smaller place in a cheaper location.

Work it right and you could retire at a younger age, as well as potentially end up with *two* homes. Sell the one large expensive home with a paid-off mortgage and buy a couple of smaller homes with lower taxes; one nearby where you used to live and the other as a winter home down south someplace nice.

Especially with returns on fixed investments being as low as they are, being mortgage-free by retirement is a key step to take.

"I don't see how you could have built up a good pension switching companies so often like that," Steve said to Harold.

"Companies? Half the time I worked for myself," Harold told him.

"But, you can't get any sort of a pension going when you're self-employed."

"Can't I? I got a pretty good one I've been dippin' into the last couple of decades. Or didn't you know that you could manage your own pension fund?"

"No... I guess I didn't," Steve said in a curious tone. "How'd you manage that one?"

Harold glanced towards the room's window, but with night still holding sway, there was really nothing out there to see, except perhaps for his own faint reflection in the windowpane.

"By recognizing the fact that the boss in question who was in charge of said pension just happened to be myself," Harold then *took a breath and turned his gaze back to Steve. "When I was growin' up, my pappy had no company to give him any pension, just his own strong back. And yet he managed to take care of himself in his fading years. Just a matter of not bein' afraid to do a couple things on your own. Now, you look like an intelligent enough youngster, think you could manage your own pension if I spelled it out for you?"*

"Before meeting you, I would have said definitely not," Steve admitted. "But now? I'm not so sure."

Harold just chuckled then explained to Steve how to go about it.

Pensions

Some people are lucky enough to get a retirement pension from the company they used to work at. Over the years the employer (and possibly the employee as well) put away some money to grow the lump sum required to fund the future pension via an insurance company. When the time comes, it will be the insurance company that your employer contracted that is making the payments to you, which will then be a combination of principal and interest. The advantage of this income stream is that you cannot outlive the payments. The disadvantage is that it stops when you die (although you can usually include a spousal contingent); but there is nothing to pass on to your heirs.

Another name for this insurance contract arrangement is "immediate annuity," which is insurance company speak for "pension plan." This name is key, though, because if your company doesn't offer a pension plan, or if you want to manage one yourself, then you can simply go to the insurance company on your own. You will just have to take a lump sum of your own savings and create a private pension by way of your own immediate annuity. The advantage of this method is that, come retirement, you can get a monthly payout of a combination of your principal and interest for as long as you and your spouse live. This way you make sure to spend all that money you saved up a little bit at a time without the fear of outliving it.

Like an employer's pension, you'll never outlive your funds with a private pension, but none of it will be passed on to your heirs.

Life Insurance

One of the best tools for your retirement plan is permanent life insurance. Yes, I've harped on the benefits of this earlier, but it's worth repeating in this context. Whether you have $400,000 or $4,000,000 saved for retirement, it is a great vehicle both for your own nest egg and to pass something onto your heirs after you pass.

Life insurance serves dual purposes. Term (temporary) insurance is true insurance; you pay a premium and hope not to need it should the insured/breadwinner die young. While this seldom happens, the income generated from the death benefit serves a very useful purpose to the survivors when they need it the most. For those people who earn less than $100,000 (so most Americans) term insurance is the way to go, as permanent insurance doesn't fit into the budget.

For those who have a retirement nest egg and assets they want to leave to others, perm (permanent) life insurance (for which there are several kinds) is the way to go. Unlike term insurance and any other insurance policy, perm insurance is guaranteed to have a claim if held until death. This, and the fact that the death benefit is income tax-free, makes it the ideal legacy transfer asset.

Ideally, people would figure this out in their 40s or 50s. Over the past several years, some of my clients have taken advantage of procuring life insurance in their retirement years for the retirement spending freedom and legacy benefit. While they no longer have the dependent income need should they die, they want the insurance as a tax efficient asset to leave to their heirs. This works for people who want to spend the principal of their retirement savings while still leaving a financial legacy behind. In a perfect world, you would obtain life insurance in an amount equal to what you want to leave your heirs. That frees you up to spend the interest and the principal of your nest egg while still leaving your heirs what you want to leave them.

Bonus points for including a long-term or chronic illness care rider, but there's more of that in the earlier chapter on insurance.

Other benefits:

- The total payments made are usually a fraction of the death benefit paid.
- The entire death benefit is received tax-free and payable in full upon the death of the insured.
- With the chronic illness rider, it's use it or keep it, meaning if the insured qualifies for the benefit and takes an advance on their death benefit, whatever they don't take is passed to their beneficiary at death.

Perm life insurance is a great way to have your cake and eat it too. You get something for your retirement, something for long-term care if you have that rider, and your heirs are still taken care of after you've passed. Even Al and Peg couldn't blow that one.

Take Advantage of What Your Employer Offers You

One key thing to be aware of is to take advantage of any benefits that your employer may offer. In a competitive economy where employers are looking for benefits they can offer to attract and keep people like you, insurance benefits rank right up there at the top of benefits to draw in top talent.

Health insurance is the first thing you want to make sure is covered, and if your employer can help you with that, then so much the better. Your options might include plans with different doctor networks. The more expensive plan usually has the better network, but you need to decide if it's worth the extra cost. Also, look at your deductible options. As I've mentioned before, I generally opt for the higher deductible plans and keep the premium savings in a liquid place (such as a Health Savings Account) for when I need those funds.

If your employer offers disability income insurance, then be very happy; if they offer to either pay for it or pay for some additional income protection, then jump on it. The odds of being disabled young are a lot higher than dying young, and that loss of income would likely be devastating. Also, if you are paying for the disability income insurance and there's a claim, the benefit payout is income tax-free. If your employer is footing the premium, the benefit would be taxable. Just make sure you are covered, as your future life plans are contingent on your income.

Life insurance options vary quite a bit from employer to employer. Many will offer a multiple of your salary as the life insurance option. This may be given to you with the option to purchase more at a very low group rate. Term insurance is very inexpensive, even more so when offered through an employer, but the reason is that you are very unlikely to have that employer's insurance when you die. It's cheap and can really help meet a need if you want to grab what you can from your employer option. Load up.

Keep in mind that your health, disability, and life insurance are not likely to go with you when you leave your employer and you may not be in as good a health later if you have to go out and procure your own insurance.

The best part of an employer benefit package is their 401k plan. You have no choice if your employer offers this plan or what options come with it. 401k plans are used for retirement because the money in them is generally penalized if withdrawn prior to age 59-and-a-half. You really have two big decisions to make: The first is how much to put in from each paycheck (typically a percentage of pay), the second being how to invest the money.

A 401k works great because you make the contributions to it directly from your paycheck and that money never makes it to your checking account. Out of sight, out of mind. Traditional 401k contributions are also income tax deductible, which is a nice up-front benefit.

When you do fund a 401k, look to see if your employer is matching a portion of any contribution made by employees. Often times your employer gives you free money to encourage you to participate in the 401k as a strong attraction and retention perk. For example, they may offer a $.50 on the dollar match of the first 6 percent of your pay that you sign up to contribute. That means your employer would add 3 percent to the 6 percent you are contributing, for a total of 9 percent. It's almost a no-brainer to do this if you can afford to do so.

Since your 401k is not liquid, you would probably want to fill your emergency fund and pay off any credit balances before committing much to your 401k. You also may want to establish some funds outside of your 401k in case you need significant money for things like a home down payment, college, or any large purchase you may have. After all, putting all your eggs in one basket is just asking for trouble should you need money for pre-retirement expenses.

Ideally you will start your 401k contributions as soon as possible, increasing them a little every year until you max out. If your employer offers a Roth 401k, you may want to contribute to that as well. Your Roth 401k contributions are not tax-deductible, but the money comes out income tax-free after 59-and-a-half.

New employer benefits to look for:

- Some employers are encouraging fitness to their employees by paying for some of their health club memberships.
- Others give rewards to employees who make their routine doctor visits every year.
- Many employers are now starting to help their employees with financial wellness by offering educational programs to help employees become aware of and understand all things finance. You should ask your human resource person about all the programs your employer offers.

"I had my mortgage paid off by the time I hit 45," Harold explained, "then spent the rest of my employment years pumping regular payments into my 401k. Twenty years later I had a nice little nest egg and no mortgage to hold me down. You'd barely notice I wasn't pulling in a regular salary anymore."

"I wish I had a set-up like that," Steve sighed.

"It's not too late, son. You still got lots of life left in you."

"This liver tells me otherwise. I'm on the waiting list, but if I don't find a transplant soon then none of what we're talking about matters a bit."

To this Harold offered no response, just lay there looking a bit thoughtful.

Highlights

- Plan for financial independence, not retirement.

- Make a list of your post-retirement monthly expenses, then compare that to your projected post-retirement income.

- The 4 percent rule is just a rule of thumb for retirement income.

- Living longer means you have to plan your finances around a longer than projected post-retirement lifetime.

- Avoid the three mistakes:

  - Retirement Euphoria

  - Failing to plan for long-term medical care

  - Relying solely on CDs and bonds in your portfolio

- If possible, pay off your mortgage before retirement.

- If you don't have a pension plan, you can create your own with an immediate annuity.

- Permanent life insurance is a great way to create a legacy asset.

~ Chapter Seven ~

Legacy Planning

Have you had the "talk?" No, not about the birds and the bees, but about a Will and your legacy. It's a hard discussion (more difficult than that other "talk"), but a necessary one. The fact is, there are a number of reasons why a lot of people keep putting off talking about the details of their will with their family:

- They don't feel it's a pressing issue.
- They are not comfortable talking openly about finances within the family.
- The kids don't want to appear greedy.
- The parents don't want their children to feel entitled to wealth.
- The parents don't want their kids to count on an inheritance (or worse yet, be in the position of having to look forward to it).

Of course, if you *don't* discuss it before it's too late, sibling feuds could erupt over what mom and dad really wanted and who gets what; it could lead to a general family-splitting nightmare. The death of a parent then becomes the death of a family. To avoid this, parents need to have a grown-up discussion with their kids about their legacy plans; discussions Beyond Money.

"Now, have you talked with your family about when you pass?" Harold asked.

"God, no," Steve replied. "I don't want to worry the kids, and there never seemed to be a right time to have this talk."

"Yet here you are, worrying about what'll happen after you cross over," Harold remarked.

"And I suppose having the talk was easy enough for you?"

"Never said it was easy, just necessary. You see, this is the sort of thing that you really only need to talk to them about once, but you do need to talk to them about it. Given that, wouldn't it be better to get it over with ahead of time then move on with the rest of your life? You do want to live, don't you?"

"Now more than ever," Steve finally admitted to himself.

"Then as soon as you're out of this hospital, you arrange to have that talk with your wife and kids. The last thing you want is everyone arguing about what you left them after you're gone. No finer way to break up a family than that."

Harold was insistent, for once not sporting his usual smile, which more than his words drove home the point that this in particular was a serious matter.

"But my kids get along great with each other."

"Sure, now. But you can't guarantee that forever. When they was young, you ever take your kids on a long car ride without at least telling them where they was goin'?"

"Of course not. They'd be quarreling before the hour would be up."

"Exactly! Now, life is a really long road trip. You don't want your kids fighting in the back seat just when you're ready to hand the wheel over to someone else, do you?"

"They'd crash the car," Steve grinned. *"I think I'm beginning to get the pattern of your metaphors."*

"It took my eldest son until he was close to 30 to catch on," Harold chuckled. *"Now he's using them on* his *kids."*

"Okay then, oh Wise One," Steve joked. *"Explain to me about legacy planning."*

"Well first, you gots to have a will, because if you don't then there might be trouble..."

What Happens If You Don't Have a Will?

What happens if there's not any will made out? Well, your assets will be distributed among your closest relatives according to your state's "intestate succession" laws. This line of succession depends on whether you're married, have kids, and various other conditions. States have varying laws about intestate succession, but here's a quick summary of the possible consequences for Illinois, at least:

131

- Children but no spouse:	The kids get everything.
- Spouse but no descendants:	The spouse gets everything.
- Spouse and descendants:	Spouse gets half of your inte tate property, descendants get the other half, with that second half being shared in equal parts by the descendants.
- Parents but no spouse, descendants or siblings:	Parents get everything.
- Siblings but no spouse, descendants, or parents:	Siblings inherit everything.
- Parents and siblings but no spouse:	Parents and siblings inherit your intestate property in equal shares, except that if only one parent is living then that parent gets a double share.

If you want to avoid this line of succession, then you need to have a will. That way you can be certain that everything goes where you want it to go.

Assets with Beneficiaries

Of course, there are many valuable assets that never get to go through a will and are not affected by intestate succession laws. This makes things simpler for those assets at least, but that's assuming that you have the paperwork on such assets up-to-date. Here are some examples of these kinds of assets:

- Property you've transferred to a living trust
- Life insurance proceeds

- Funds in an IRA, 401k, or other retirement account
- Securities held in a transfer-on-death account
- Real estate held by a transfer-on-death deed
- Payable-on-death bank accounts
- Property you own with someone else in a joint tenancy or tenancy by the entirety

Each of these types of assets will pass to the living co-owner or beneficiary who you have named in the records for that asset. Of course, this assumes that such records are up-to-date. For instance, you may have survived a beneficiary, or maybe you're rethinking whether a now-married child should be a beneficiary because you'd rather their spouse not get half of it if they divorce.

If no beneficiary is mentioned for any of these types of assets, then they will pass through your will, which means they may be subject to estate taxes (and no one likes those!), which brings you back to having that "talk" with your family.

What if you're worried that a beneficiary might predecease you, or disclaim their portion? Then you can add a "per stirpes" designation, which means that the assets would then pass on in equal shares to their own descendants. You can also name a "contingent beneficiary," so that if the beneficiary dies before you do, there's another person listed to receive the account.

If you're married, then you can avoid the will by designating your spouse as a "joint owner" of these assets with "rights of survivorship." This way, when you pass, the person so-named just has to submit proof of death and they take over as the individual owner.

What if you're single? Then you can include a "transfer on death" clause, specifying a secondary owner who will be the new owner of the assets at your death.

Finally, if you really want to avoid going through a will, then you could set up all your taxable assets in a living trust, but that's the more expensive route to take.

Whatever you do, keep records of all your assets, and keep them together in a place where the executor won't be having to go on a treasure hunt trying to find them.

"I been checkin' my will, oh, every once in a while," Harold told Steve. "Just in case things change."

"What could change? You still have the same number of kids, I'm guessing."

"Well, here's an example of a change I wanted." Harold started. "My son Billy been doin' a lot to help take care of me and my wife the last several years, so I figured he ought to get a little somethin' extra; jus' my way of sayin' thanks. Even talked to the other kids about it and they all agreed. And there's the fact that I've also outlived two prospective executors."

"Two of them?"

"It's that southern tea. Even if it's not good for what ails ya', it makes it bearable enough to keep on hangin' in."

"I'm starting to believe that," Steve grinned. "But seriously, how bad could it get if you don't keep your will updated?"

"*Pretty serious,*" Harold replied. "*I knew this one fine woman, and her husband had one of those progressive diseases that just got worse and worse over the years until he was nearly like a skeleton when he passed. Her son was there to help 'em out, while the daughter went about getting her own life. Which was fine. Well, after 25 years the guy passed, then the son took it upon himself to stay on and look after his mother. Good thing too, because after a few years she got sick, and he was there as usual. Sure, the daughter came in for a bit every now and then, but that boy was there for her up until the very minute that she passed.*"

"*Sounds like he should have gotten a medal.*"

"*You'd think that, but no. There was a will alright, but it was 30 years old; written well before anyone knew how bad that husband's disease would get or how much of his life the son would devote to caring for the two of 'em. The daughter just figured her brother had been lazing around the house the entire time and ended up dragging him through probate court for six entire years. Wasted a lot of time and money and nearly broke the poor kid.*"

"*My God, and they were brother and sister? That's it, I'm getting my will updated the minute I'm out of here. I don't want my kids ending up like that.*"

"*That, son, is probably the best decision you've come to yet. No one should go through something like that if there's any other way around it...*"

Keep Your Will Updated

First obvious question: How long ago was your will drafted, and does it need updating? (We're skipping past the "Do I really need a will" question, because you *do*.)

There are a number of things that could have changed since the last time you looked at everything. You may have divorced and remarried, had some new kids since the last time you looked at your will, maybe some grandkids, or perhaps something else changed? That descendant of yours who was married and had a good job, who you thought would never need as much as his siblings, may have lost his job, gotten divorced, and really be hurting. Would it be fair then for him to get less because the last time you looked at your will was back in the "good times?" Or perhaps you've been going through years of a chronic illness and there was that one child who stuck around to take care of you; you might want to reward him a bit more than the others.

Although you may have changed your mind since the last time you looked at everything, the courts have to go by what you have *written down*, so you had better make sure the information in your will is up-to-date and matches your wishes. If there have been a few changes in your life that might affect your legacy, then it might be time to take a quick look-see into what you have recorded.

Here's a few things to keep in mind when you review your legacy plans:

- Check the date. How current is your will compared to significant events in your life?

- Update the will and any trusts you might have to reflect the current financial condition of your children (and grandchildren, if appropriate). Who *really* looks like he might need a little help in the future?

- Is there anyone who went through extraordinary lengths to assist you in something since the last time you looked things over? Someone that you want to ensure will be compensated?

- If you plan on giving a large amount of money to charity, then your children could feel slighted and disappointed, or maybe even unloved after you're gone. Discuss ahead of time the reasons why you are naming that charity in your will.

- If any beneficiaries or people named in the will, such as guardians or the executor, have already passed, then you need to update those entries. Or maybe you've changed your mind on the executor or guardian (a proposed guardian for your kids might have moved out of state, for instance).

- Above all, make sure that it is as easy as possible for the executor to locate all account and asset information. As uncomfortable as it might be to run him through it while you're still alive, things could turn into a logistical nightmare once you've passed and he doesn't know where anything is. Maybe at least include a note or something along with the will; everything in the same folder to make it easy for him to find it all.

137

Planning for College for the Yet-To-Be-Born

I've mentioned 529 college savings plans before, but did you know that you can use them as a part of your estate planning?

College expenses are on an unending spiral skyward, but you can hedge against these costs by funding a 529 account for your grandkids before your *children* are even ready for college. 529 accounts continue to grow tax-free as long as you only use the funds for qualified school expenses. If you really need to withdraw money for any other reason, though (like an emergency), you can do that but will have to pay income taxes on the earned portion of it and a 10 percent federal penalty. That aside, though, here's how it can help you out.

Beneficiaries of a 529 plan can use the money for any college they care to choose, but even if the child named as a beneficiary decides not to attend college, you can still change the beneficiary at will, or even fund your own continuing education. While you are alive you retain control of the money and who it goes to at any given time. If you pass away before all this is used up, however, you can name a successor owner—say your child or grandchild—in which case that person takes over the account with *their* child as the beneficiary.

A 529 college savings plan has a number of investment options and tax benefits, which I touched upon briefly in an earlier chapter. If you want to ensure your family's education as a part of your legacy, then the 529 plan is your best option.

"So, you've had your grandkids' college funded for before they were even born?" Steve was amazed. "Man, now that's planning!"

"That's all it takes, is a little planning. No reason why anyone should end up poor and destitute jus' when life's starting to get good."

"Well, I've got to admit, you certainly gave me a lot to think about, Harold."

"Glad I could help. Now if you don't mind I'd like to rest up a bit to be ready for my family. They're due in about an hour."

That's when Steve realized just how long they'd been talking. Morning had been leaking in through the windows for at least an hour, and for the first time in a very long while, he was starting to notice just how gorgeous the sunrise can look.

Highlights

- You need a will.

- Without a will, assets get divided according to intestate succession laws.

- Some types of assets have their own beneficiaries named, bypassing the need for going through a will.

- Keep your asset beneficiary records up-to-date.

- Keep your will up-to-date based on what has changed in your life.

- Make sure that any beneficiaries and other persons named in the will are also up-to-date.

- Make it easy for the executor to locate all needed asset account information.

- Discuss the reasons for some of your decisions, such as charitable donations, with your children.

- A 529 college savings plan can be the perfect way to provide education to your legacy.

Chapter Eight

Your Financial Wellness

———————⌁———————

Harold's family arrived soon after, crowding around the old man with tears, well-wishes, and hopeful looks. Seventeen people—kids, grandkids, and his wife—all gathered there to say their good-byes. There were many tearful faces, more than a few jokes and laughter bandying about, but little of what Steve would term as true sorrow. Many people said phrases like, "We'll miss you, Granpa." His kids and grandkids took turns holding his hand, but through it all Steve saw one thing lacking, and he found its absence quite unusual.

There was no worry on Harold's face; there was only joy and contentment, for he had seen to it all and knew that all his loved ones would be taken care of. He had led a good life, and there was nothing that wasn't taken care of that would worry him. The Lord had also promised him that with his Faith came Eternal life.

Seeing the tears as they flowed, the happiness on Harold's face to be surrounded by all his loved ones in his final hours, sparing the occasional wink in Steve's direction, it finally sank in. Steve watched and finally he knew.

All this time, Steve had been planning for his death, while Harold had been living his life. The death came anyway, but it was what passed before that mattered. You needn't sacrifice the living of life to lead a successful one, not if you plan ahead and lead a life of balance and financial wellness.

Later that day Steve found he was to be discharged to a hospice for care. He went back to his old room to check up on Harold, but the old man had passed away peacefully in his sleep... with a smile on his face.

The next morning Steve received a phone call: A last-minute liver transplant had become available for him. It seemed he would have a second chance at life.

"I promise, old man," he said to himself after receiving the news. "I'll do things different. Just as you taught me. I'll plan ahead and live for Life, not Death. It's not too late."

Now that we have the pieces, let's pull it all together. From the basics to the cap on it all, I have arranged this book like a pyramid. Chapter One is the basis upon which all else is built, the foundation to your financial wellness, while Chapter Seven is the crown, the final element. That's not to say that you can't start organizing more than one of these sections at the same time, but make sure that your foundations are covered first.

Step One: Get Hold of Your Life–Beyond Money

Before you can begin with anything, you have got to get a handle on your spending. I detailed it all in Chapter One, but the basic message is this: You must ensure that your incoming funds are greater than your outgoing, or you will never be able to make any savings or investment plan work. Limit your credit card purchases; no more impulse buying, and keep out-of-pocket spending to what is literally just in your pocket. Living efficiently and on a budget doesn't mean you have to have less of what life brings you.

For couples, you both have to be on the same page when it comes to money-matters. Stay in communication, and stick to that budget and those savings goals you've both planned on. Of course, single or married, having a budget doesn't mean that you can't program in some fun and family time; just don't go hog-wild with the checkbook approach to vacation time.

Step Two: Start Saving Now

A good time to start on a savings plan is the minute you have money to save, which is why you've got to master Step One first so that moment in time arrives all the quicker. With each paycheck, set aside your weekly allowance and stick to it, then partition off a set portion of that check into what you need for your savings and investment plans, your bills, and emergency fund. Automatic savings transfers will ensure that you have everything set aside before bad spending habits get in the way. And remember that you want to have a low mortgage payment relative to your income and have it paid off by retirement.

- Set aside money for your emergency fund.
- Set aside your weekly allowance and *no more.*
- Budget your bills.

Step Three: Insure So the Future Doesn't Catch You Off Guard

Now that you've begun to start setting some money aside, you can climb up to the next level of the pyramid. Insurance can be an important hedge against an unkind future, especially if you have a family. But you have to know what the best type of insurance is for your situation. Coordinate your deductibles with your emergency fund, and make sure that you are insured for what you *will* need: those things that, while unlikely, could be *very* expensive.

When it comes to medical and life insurance, don't forget that you're also thinking of your family. Make sure that it's not only a plan that fits you and your needs, but will also be there for your loved ones many years down the line. Make sure to have adequate disability income and life insurance since your entire family's financial future is predicated on this. Term life is fine if that's all you can afford, but ideally get some permanent life insurance. Make sure you and your loved ones have a financial plan that won't fall apart should you die young or become disabled.

Remember:

- Review your vehicle and home insurance periodically.
- Save money with higher deductibles; you don't need insurance for small out-of-pocket expenses.
- Save on medical insurance by using a high deductible for what is unpredictable, unlikely to happen, and really expensive.
- Study carefully the options for projected long-term care funding solutions.

Step Four: Understand Your Investment Options, and Don't Go at It Like an Amateur

When I speak about being an "amateur," I mean for you to remember my lecture on "greed and fear" and the damage that mindset can do to your investment scheme. You've changed your lifestyle and started to save up some money; now it's time to step up another level of the pyramid and start planning for the long-term. But, before you take the leap into investing, understand what you're getting into. Understand the differences between stocks and bonds, between active and passive investing, and determine which investment strategy makes sense for *your* situation. Know the field before you play the game, and remember to ask yourself this all-important question: How much can I afford to lose on paper before I start panic-selling? Diversify your portfolio to be aligned with your tolerance for volatility. Professional guidance may be very prudent for this.

Plan your portfolio around your current resources, your future needs, and what you feel that you can manage. Then don't forget to keep an eye on it through the years.

Step Five: Make Sure to Consider Investment Taxes

Still on the same level of the pyramid as investments come the taxes on those investments. Remember the first rule of investing: It's not what you make that matters, but what you keep. There are a lot of investment possibilities out there, but some of them end up not looking so pretty once you figure in those investment taxes. A Roth 401k, for instance, has several tax advantages over a regular 401k, while mutual funds could pass on unexpected taxes.

Then there are some zero investment tax investment vehicles that help you save for your kids' college funds, health plans, and even life insurance. Investments are a great way of planning for the future; being able to *keep* a majority of that money once you get there is even better. Plan carefully to be as tax efficient as possible.

Step Six: Plan for Retirement

Two things to keep in mind here. First, the best time to start planning for retirement is *right now*. Second, you are *not* planning for your retirement but for your financial independence. You are planning for the day when you won't have to work to thrive, when you can get more enjoyment out of life without punching a time clock. You aren't planning for the day that you die, but the day that you simply move onto a new phase in your life.

Plan ahead for what you might need when you get there:

- Take steps to allow for possible long-term medical care.
- Make sure your mortgage will be paid off.
- Do not rely solely on CDs and bonds to generate retirement income.
- Avoid the mistake of "Retirement Euphoria."
- Make sure you know what your savings investments will *really* be paying you upon retirement. Will it be enough for the longer lives that people are living nowadays?
- Start plotting for your retirement income plan the first day you start work.

Step Seven: Protect Your Legacy

No one likes to talk about the day they will no longer be around, but it's a talk that you must have. Get the ball rolling now and you won't have to waste all those years worrying about it. Protecting your legacy is basically just a matter of record keeping; once you set it up, the rest is just a matter of re-checking it from time to time to make sure that your plans are up-to-date with your current reality. For this final level of the pyramid, once you have everything else below it running like a well-oiled machine, this part becomes the simplest of all, though the most critical:

- Get a will, and keep it up-to-date.
- Keep your asset records up-to-date.

- Don't be afraid to discuss all your plans with your family and loved ones. Get their input.

- Make sure that all beneficiaries and persons named in your will are still current. Has anyone pre-deceased you? Is the executor you named still a viable option?

- Make it easy for your executor to locate everything that he will need.

Your financial wellness is my concern, and it should be yours, too. That is why I have written this book, to make it as simple and straightforward as I can for you to get started, get your finances under control, and start planning for life. Too often people struggle their entire lives with their finances. Never having a plan or figuring out that money is just a tool. Take time to figure out what your goals are, prioritize them, and align your money accordingly. Save to improve the quality of your life and that of your family. And finally, enjoy your life... just don't let the finances get out of control or fail to have contingencies in place to prevent something from turning into a financial disaster that could ruin your life.

A properly built financial plan is as stable as a pyramid, and it will serve you and yours for generations to come—Beyond Money.

It was many years later. Now Steve's kids were grown and out of college with their own children. The combination of the new liver and following of Harold's advice had led Steve down a path where he'd found both the time and resources to enjoy his

life and his family. He'd made his plans, seen to his children and grandchildren, and taken care of such details as he and his wife would need in their fading years.

In short, he was happy and content.

It was on the eve of his 70th birthday that he received a strange letter hand-delivered by a special courier. Strange because it had been mailed 22 years earlier.

"It's from someone named Harold Ramses," his wife said as she walked it over to him.

Steve shook his head. He stared at the envelope for over a minute. Then, like seeing a rainbow for the first time, a warm glow welled up inside of him, and a beaming smile grew over his face.

"Harold?!" He nearly shouted. "But it can't *be. You remember that old man that spoke to me back in the hospital?"*

"That Harold? But Steve, why would he send a letter to be delivered 22 years later?"

"He must have written it shortly before he passed. I wonder what he has to say."

It was eager fingers that tore open the old letter, Steve more curious than his wife to see what parting words the old man from the hospital had to say, What advice from beyond the grave. It read:

Steve, happy 70th birthday. Or at least it'd better be because I paid the man enough to make sure that's when you'll receive this.

I'm guessing by now that you've had plenty of time to turn things around, so congratulations on all the success. Your family's all taken care of, and you've had a chance to learn to finally enjoy your life. I just wanted to leave you with one last nugget of wisdom…

"I only knew the man for something like three hours," Steve chuckled, "and he's still giving me advice long after his death."

"Do you plan on ignoring it?" his wife asked.

"At this point? Heck no. Let's see what he has to say."

The one very important thing you need to know at 70 is that your life is never over with. Anyone who plans for death will find it a lot faster than otherwise. Like my pappy used to say, "You only find the things you're looking for." So, what is it that YOU are looking for? Whatever it is, I hope that you keep on finding it. Live with joy in your heart always.

By the way, I hope your new liver's working good…. And, well, I guess I won't be using it anymore. It's the one thing in me still working right, so why waste it, right?

-Harold Ramses.

"That man gave me more than a new life. He gave me life itself. Honey? Remember that trip to Greece we spoke about?"

"Yeah, sure, but I've not checked that savings account for six months."

"Look in your desk drawer," Steve smirked.

As Nancy slowly opened the desk drawer, she expected to see two tickets for a cruise around the Greek islands. They had dreamed about it for years, but she had always thought it would remain just a dream.

When she opened the drawer all the way, she saw there was an envelope there from the cruise line but it did not contain two tickets.

As tears welled up in Nancy's eyes, Steve held her by his side. Harold's advice had more than paid off. Steve was given not just a second chance but dozens of chances. He had not only turned around their financial wellness, but in so doing, he had made the best investment of his life.

He had invested and continued to invest in the one area that meant the most: his family.

The envelope had six tickets; one for Nancy, Steve, Sara, Jack, Katie, and one more person, Katie's fiancé!

Looks like Steve would be dancing at Katie's (fully-funded) wedding after all, and in Greece. Steve and Nancy had truly learned some timeless wisdom... Beyond Money.

Made in the USA
Columbia, SC
19 February 2023

12508243R00098